Elegant Everyday Cooking

Maria E. Gray

www.youtube.com/ilovetocookalot

Elegant Everyday Cooking

ISBN: 978-0-9848877-0-5

For Jessica Anne

Contents

FORWARD 12

APPETIZERS 14

BABA GHANOUJ - EGGPLANT DIP 16

CALIFORNIA ROLL 18

CHEESE SABLES 19

CRAB CAKES 21

CROSTINI 22

TOMATO, BASIL AND GARLIC TOPPING 22

ROASTED GARLIC WITH BAKED BRIE 24

MINI GOUGERES 25

GUACOMOLE 26

ROASTED STUFFED MUSHROOMS 27

HUMMUS 29

PALMIERS 31

PARMESAN CHEESE CRISPS (FRICO) 33

PARMESAN CHEESE PUFF PASTRY STRAWS 34

PESTO 35

PICO DI GALLO 36

PROSCIUTTO WRAPPED FIGS STUFFED WITH
MOZZARELLA 37

ROAST BEEF SPIRALS 38

EASY PITA CHIPS 39

TORTELLINI SKEWERS 40

www.youtube.com/ilovetocookalot

TZATZKI...41

BREADS...42

BANANA BREAD 43

BEER BREAD 45

BUTTERMILK SKILLET CORN BREAD.................46

IRISH SODA BREAD.................................47

ONION SESAME BREAD 49

PITA BREAD 51

WHITE BREAD 53

SALADS...54

ARTICHOKE AND ASPARAGUS SALAD.............55

ARUGULA, BACON AND APPLE SALAD.............57

BLACK BEAN AND PEPPER SALAD 58

CAPRESE SALAD......................................59

CHICKPEA SALAD 60

CORN AND LIME SALAD.............................62

CUCUMBER SALAD 63

COLD NOODLE SALAD 64

GOAT CHEESE SALAD 65

JELLO FRUIT MOLD..................................67

JICAMA AND ORANGE SALAD 69

CLASSIC MACARONI SALAD 70

MANGO BERRY SALAD WITH GINGER 71

MILLET SALAD...72

PASTA SALAD WITH TRI-COLOR ROASTED PEPPERS 73

POTATO SALAD – GERMAN STYLE......................74

SHRIMP, VEGGIE AND NOODLE DINNER SALAD 75

TROPICAL FRUIT SALAD 77

PINEAPPLE BOAT FRUIT SALAD...........................78

ROASTED VEGGIE TRI COLORED SALAD...........80

SPINACH SALAD 82

THREE BEAN SALAD..83

WALDORF SALAD..84

WATERMELON SALAD 85

WILD RICE SALAD..86

SOUPS 87

ASPARAGUS SOUP..88

AVOCADO SOUP 90

MINESTRONE..91

CREAM OF CELERY SOUP....................................93

LIONS HEAD SOUP..95

MUSHROOM SOUP 97

OYSTER PAN ROAST 98

SPLIT PEA SOUP 100

PORK STEW WITH VEGGIES AND DUMPLINGS102

SHRIMP NOODLE BOWL..104

WHITE BEAN SOUP 106

WEDDING SOUP 108

VEGGIES, SIDES, PASTA AND RICE 110

STUFFED ARTICHOKES 111

ROASTED BEETS 112

BABY BOK CHOY WITH GARLIC 113

CUBAN STYLE BLACK BEANS 114

CREAMED SPINACH 115

STEAMED BROCOLLI 116

BRUSSELS SPROUTS 117

CREPES WITH SPICED APPLE FILLING 118

EGGPLANT PARMIGAN 120

FRITTATA 122

GNOCCHI VERDI 124

FRESH PASTA 126

SOFT POLENTA WITH CHEESE 127

MASHED POTATOES WITH GREEN OLIVES AND
CREAM CHEESE 128

POTATOES AND CAULIFLOWER WITH INDIAN
SPICES 129

POTATO GRATIN 131

ROYAL RICE 132

WHITE RISOTTO 133

ROASTED GREEN BEANS AND CARROTS WITH
BALSAMIC HONEY GLAZE 134

SEVEN VEGETABLE STIR FRY 135

TEX MEX RICE 137

MAIN DISHES 138

BEEF AND BROCOLLI 139

BI BIM BOP 141

BURRITO – CALIFORNIA STYLE 143

CAULIFLOWER CHEESE TART WITH
CARMELIZED ONIONS 145

CHILI VERDE 147

PERFECT ROAST CHICKEN 149

CHICKEN AL MATTONE (Flattened Chicken) 151

CHICKEN CORDON BLEU 152

CHICKEN CUTLETS WITH GARLIC CHARD AND
SPAGHETTI SQUASH 154

CHICKEN PICATTA 156

CHICKEN STUFFED WITH FETA AND SPINACH
....158

SYRIAN CHICKEN 160

STUFFED GRAPE LEAVES 162

HAM AND NOODLE CASSEROLE 164

LASAGNA AL FORNO 165

GRILLED HERB CRUSTED LAMB 168

LEEK AND CHEESE PIE 169

MEATBALLS 170

JERK CHICKEN 171

PORK TENDERLOIN WITH THYME SALT CRUST 173

PIZZA 174

VEAL SALTIMBOCA 176

SALMON CAKES...178

SHEPARDS PIE 180

SOUTHERN FRIED CHICKEN 182

THE PERFECT STEAK 183

PEPPERCORN MARINATED FLANK STEAK 184

CHEESE AND SPINACH RAVIOLI 186

TUNA NOODLE CASSEROLE 188

VEGETABLE CURRY 190

VEAL AND MUSHROOM COBBLER 192

VEAL CANNELONI..195

SHOW STOPPER MAINS...197

CRISPY FRAGRANT DUCK..............................198

PIEROGI 201

BEEF WELLINGTONS 204

TIMPANO 207

THANKSGIVING...211

PUMPKIN PIE...213

SPICED CRANBERRY SAUCE 214

CANDIED SWEET POTATOES 215

CHESTNUT SAUSAGE APPLE STUFFING...........216

www.youtube.com/ilovetocookalot

GLORIOUS ROAST TURKEY 218

DESSERT 220

    ALMOND BISCOTTI 222

    AMBROSIA..224

    ANGEL FOOD CAKE 225

    APRICOT ALMOND TART............................226

    APPLE CRISP 228

    BISCOTTI DI REGINA 230

    BLUEBERRY PIE WITH STARS 231

    BUTTERSCOTCH PUDDING 233

    MINI CARROT CUPCAKES 234

    CHEESECAKE – NEW YORK STYLE...................236

    CHERRY COOKIES 238

    CHOCOLATE BISCOTTI 239

    DARK CHOCOLATE BROWNIES 241

    CHOCOLATE CRINKLE COOKIES....................243

    CHOCOLATE PUDDING 245

    DARK CHOCOLATE TRUFFLE.............................247

    CHURROS...248

    BAKED EGG CUSTARD 250

    FLAN 251

    FORTUNE COOKIES.....................................253

    ICE CREAM 255

    JELLY ROLL 257

LEMON PIE 259

MADELEINES 261

PINEAPPLE UPSIDE DOWN CAKE 262

RAINBOW COOKIES 264

PEARS POACHED IN MARSALA WINE 266

POUND CAKE..268

RICE PUDDING...269

TARTE TATIN..270

STRAWBERRY RHUBARB PIE 272

ITAILIAN CHEESECAKE 273

TAPIOCA PUDDING 275

OATMEAL LACE COOKIES 276

PANNA COTTA...277

RASBERRY OR BLACKBERRY COULIS..............278

FLOATING ISLANDS.................................279

STRAWBERRY SORBET 281

MENU IDEAS FROM THE RECIPES IN THIS BOOK
....282

FORWARD

This is a real cook book, not a coffee table book. It contains a collection of recipes for everyday cooking. It is not exhaustive, or laden with technique or culinary history or facts. It is simply a sampling of the dishes I actually make for my family on a regular basis, and suggestions for how to pair them.

Preparing a home cooked meal for family and friends is a wonderful labor of love. Cooking from scratch affords me full control over the quality of food we eat and share with others. I love to cook, and I enjoy creating and refining recipes to produce great tasting food that's good for my family as well. It's easy to choose ingredients that benefit your health. I always try to stick with organic produce and meats. Olive oil and canola oil are wonderful oils, and a little whole milk or butter are all it takes to add flavor to dishes. Some ingredients, such as light sour cream, don't suffer in their reduced fat incarnation. Some recipes can be streamlined with no harm to the end result, and even, on occasion show improvement. Homemade ice cream and panna cotta both work wonderfully well with low fat milk in place of heavy cream, as an example.

Pairing appetizers, sides and main dishes in a way that is colorful almost guarantees a successful outcome. Vegetables don't need a lot of elaborate preparation to taste and look beautiful. Appetizers are fun and can be a very elegant part of any meal. Never forget dessert - a simple piece of ripe perfect fruit can be a fabulous ending

www.youtube.com/ilovetocookalot

to any meal, but homemade desserts are always well received and many can be done ahead.

I share here a few of my favorite recipes for appetizers, breads, side dishes, salads, main dishes and desserts. At the end of the book I include several menus drawing on the recipes herein. I wish you good health and happy cooking!

APPETIZERS

Appetizers - hors d'oeuvres... those cute little bites of food, elegant or amusing and almost always tiny - they're just plain fun. They can serve many purposes; to stimulate the appetite, to help anticipate the main meal, all on their own as the meal, or aiding absorption of alcohol in cocktails. Rich finger foods can aid a cocktail party or after work get together for drinks with friends. Appetizers can serve as a prelude to a formal meal, and allow the cook to attend to last minute preparations.

In general, you want your appetizers to complement your main meal - either stay with one type of ethnic cuisine or mix lighter appetizers with a more robust meal or go the other way round.

Talk of appetizers conjures up images of shrimp cocktail, finger sandwiches, and little skewers of all kinds. Crudités and dip, chips and dip are also popular - but don't be limited by these alone. Often, simple preparations can be amazing, and many appetizers are do ahead deals - presentation, as always with food, is key and can add a depth of sophistication to even the easiest spread.

I love to serve crostini topped with a variety of toppings (but limit it to two or three types on a platter, and never over crowd my serving platter). Baked brie with roasted garlic is always fun. Make ahead appetizers like palmiers, parmesan pastry straws and frico are big on the "wow" factor. My twice roasted mushrooms take stuffed mushrooms to a new level. Try pairing some homemade

www.youtube.com/ilovetocookalot

tzatzki and hummus with easy pita chips. You can always add a platter of veggies and dip – different colored peppers are great to showcase more labor intensive appetizers.

Some nights I make a dinner out of assorted "ethnic" appetizers. The Spanish do Tapas, Greeks do a mezzo platter, and the Italians have their antipasto. Really you can put any set of appetizers together that complement one another and have a wonderful fun dinner. The classic cocktail party takes this approach, and appetizers can be served without a formal setting or even any seating!

BABA GHANOUJ - EGGPLANT DIP

This delightful dip pairs well with Mediterranean food. Serve it with pita wedges, veggies to dip or on roasted meat.

Ingredients

- 3 medium eggplants (about 2 lbs)
- 1 Tbs olive oil
- 1 large vidalla onion, chopped
- 1/2 tsp salt
- 3 cloves minced garlic
- 1 minced shallot (optional)
- juice of 1-3 lemons
- 2 Tbs tahini paste
- flat leaf parsley, for garnish

www.youtube.com/ilovetocookalot

Directions

Preheat oven to 400 F. Prick eggplants with a fork in a few places and place on baking sheet and bake for about 1 hour, or until tender. Remove and let cool. Heat olive oil in a cast iron skillet and add chopped onion, sprinkle with salt and cook over medium low flame stirring occasionally for about 30 mins, add minced garlic and shallot and continue to cook stirring frequently for another 10-15 mins, or until reduced down and caramelized. Cut eggplants in half and remove flesh, discarding dark black seeds. Mash eggplant flesh in a small bowl. Add onion mixture to eggplants, add lemon juice and tahini and mash with a potato masher, or process in a food processor if a smoother texture is desired. Serve at room temperature.

CALIFORNIA ROLL

Easy to assemble and fun to eat, these pretty sushi inspired rolls look beautiful arranged on a colorful platter. No raw fish to worry about in this recipe.

Ingredients

- 1 cup sushi rice (short grain rice)
- 1.25 cups water
- 2 Tbs rice vinegar
- 1/2 English cucumber, cut into long thin strips
- 1/2 avocado cut into thin strips
- 1 tsp sesame seeds
- 1 tsp pickled ginger
- 1 tsp wasabi powder + 1 tsp water
- 2 tbs imitation crab meat
- 2 - 3 sheets nori seafood vegetable

Directions

Rinse rice in cold water until water runs clear, drain. Combine rice and water in a pot and bring to a boil. Cover and lower heat, simmer for 20 mins. Leave covered for 5-10 mins. Turn rice into a nonmetallic bowl and stir in rice vinegar. Let cool. Place a sheet of nori, shiny side down on sushi mat covered with plastic wrap. Place a single layer of rice all over nori, leaving a 1" border on far side. In the middle layer cucumber, avocado, sesame seeds, ginger and crab meat - dot with wasabi paste first if desired. Roll up tightly. Cut into rolls with a knife dipped in cold water.

www.youtube.com/ilovetocookalot

CHEESE SABLES

Butter, flakey and wonderful little crackers. You can cut these in seasonal shapes – leaves or pumpkins for fall, stars and moons for fun, hearts for valentines day etc. These are delicious served with a bowl of grapes, and you can make them ahead. They only take about 10 mins to bake and make quite an impressive appetizer.

Ingredients

- 5 Tbs unsalted butter, cut into small cubes and placed in the freezer for 15 mins
- 1 cup all-purpose unbleached flour
- ½ tsp salt
- 1 tsp paprika
- 8 oz grated gruyere cheese
- ¼ cup ice cold water

Directions

Preheat oven to 375 F. Combine flour and salt in food processor. Pulse in butter. Pulse in cheese. Add cold water, 1 Tbs at a time, into a ball of dough forms. Turn out onto lightly floured board and form into a ball then flatten into a disc. Can cover in plastic wrap and refrigerate for up to a day, if desired, remove from refrigerator 30 mins before rolling. Roll dough to ¼ inch thickness and cut out 2" shapes. Place on parchment lined

www.youtube.com/ilovetocookalot

baking sheets and cover and refrigerate at least 30 mins and up to overnight. Remove plastic wrap and brush with egg yolk beaten with 1 Tbs cold water. Sprinkle with parmesan, or poppy seeds, or additional paprika. Bake for 10-15 mins or until golden. Remove to wire rack and let cool.

CRAB CAKES

These are great if you make them rather petite (about 1.5 " in diameter) to serve as finger food, or make them larger and serve as a first course on a bed of greens or as a light lunch.

Ingredients

- 6 oz of fresh lump crab meat, picked over to remove any shells
- 1.5-2 Tbs low fat mayonnaise
- 1/2-1 tsp old bay seasoning
- 3 Tbs chopped fresh parsley
- 1/4 cup seasoned breadcrumbs
- 2 Tbs olive oil or butter

Directions

Combine mayonnaise with old bay seasoning, add crab meat add parsley and breadcrumbs. Form into patties and pat some more breadcrumbs on each side of each patty. Cover and refrigerate for at least 1 hour and up to overnight. Melt butter or heat oil in a cast iron skillet, over medium heat fry crab cakes turning once after about 2-3 mins. Serve hot.

CROSTINI

A simple yet very versatile dish, crostini can be prepared ahead and stored in an air tight container for up to a week. These are great to have on hand for impromptu entertaining. Top them with ricotta or goats cheese and garnish with a slice of fresh basil and freshly ground black pepper. Top with an olive or mushroom tapenade, or with my favorite, tomato and garlic topping.

Ingredients

- 1 slender french baguette
- 1 clove garlic, peeled and halved
- 2 Tbs olive oil
- 1 tsp herbs de province
- 1 tsp sea salt
- freshly ground black pepper

Directions

Cut bread into 1/2 inch slices and rub each slice with the cut surface of the garlic. Combine the oil with herbs, salt and pepper and brush both sides of each bread slice lightly. Lay flat on a baking sheet and bake for 10 mins in a 350 oven. Cool on a wire rack.

TOMATO, BASIL AND GARLIC TOPPING

Ingredients

- 6-8 baby roma tomatoes
- 2 cloves chopped garlic
- 3 fresh basil leaves, chopped
- 1 Tbs olive oil
- salt
- freshly ground black pepper

Directions

Bring a pot of water to a boil. Cut a small x in the end of the tomatoes (not the stem end) plunge tomatoes into boiling water for 20 sec. drain and cool briefly. Peel tomatoes, chop finely and discard seeds and peel. Combine tomatoes, garlic, basil, olive oil and salt and pepper in a small bowl. Top crostini with a tsp or two of mixture and garnish platter with basil sprigs.

ROASTED GARLIC WITH BAKED BRIE

Easy and elegant. Roasting garlic transforms it into a buttery, mellow spread. Serve with crostini or fresh Italian bread slices.

Ingredients

- 2 heads garlic, slice 1/3 of top off
- 1 Tbs olive oil
- 1 wedge brie cheese
- 1 small French bread

Directions

Place cut heads of whole garlic in foil, drizzle with olive oil wrap in foil and bake for about 1 hour at 400 F. Add brie or brie like cheese in a small cast iron skillet to oven for about 5 mins or until cheese barely begins to melt. Slice bread and serve with garlic and cheese.

MINI GOUGERES

These delightful, mouthwatering cheese pastries are based on the classic choux pastry. You can vary the flavor by changing the cheese, maybe mild cheddar for children for example.

Ingredients

- 3/4 cup water
- 1/2 tsp salt
- 3 Tbs unsalted butter
- 3/4 cup flour
- 3 eggs
- 1.5 cups grated gruyere cheese (or other hard cheese)

Directions

Combine water, salt and butter in a medium pan over high heat. Bring to a boil. Remove from heat and add the flour stirring constantly until combined. Return pan to low heat and stir well until mixture is smooth and pulls away from the sides of the pan. Remove from heat, add eggs - one at a time, stirring vigorously after each addition, beat until mixture is smooth and glossy. Add cheese and stir to incorporate. Drop by teaspoonfuls on a greased baking sheet and at 350 for 30 mins. Serve warm. You can bake these ahead and freeze for up to 3 months, then defrost and crisp in a preheated 400 oven for 3 mins.

GUACOMOLE

Classic and easy this avocado dip goes well with chips of course, but it also makes a great sandwich spread. Use it as a dip with corn chips, or inside a burrito or as a topper for Mexican rice and beans.

Ingredients

- 3-4 medium ripe haas avocados
- juice from 1 lime
- 1 tsp sea salt
- 1/4 cup chopped cilantro
- medium tomato, diced and squeezed to remove excess water and seeds

Directions

Cut avocados down the middle and twist to separate into halves. Remove pit and reserve,
remove flesh to a medium bowl. Add lime juice and salt and use a fork to coarsely mash the avocado. Add cilantro and stir to combine. Place a reserved pit or two on top of guacamole and cover with plastic wrap. Refrigerate for about an hour. Remove pit before serving and garnish with a sprig of cilantro if desired.

ROASTED STUFFED MUSHROOMS

*Wonderfully decadent twice roasted mushrooms with bacon and feta –
these never fail to wow! What's equally wonderful is the do ahead
capability – allowing you to have them ready to pop in the oven just
before guests arrive!*

Ingredients

- 8 slices bacon, reserve 1 Tbs bacon fat
- 18 white mushrooms (about 2" in diameter)
- 18 cremini mushrooms (about 2" in diameter)
- 1 cup finely chopped onion
- 1/4 cup olive oil
- 4 oz feta cheese crumbles
- 3 oz cream cheese at room temperature
- 7 oz baby spinach, cooked and drained and chopped
- 1/2 tsp crushed red pepper
- salt and pepper

Directions

Saute onion in bacon fat until golden. Drain and combine
with spinach, cream cheese, feta, crumbled bacon, red
pepper and salt and pepper to taste. Toss mushrooms in 1/4
cup olive oil and season with salt and pepper. Place
rounded sides down in a single layer on a foil lined baking
sheet and cook at 375 for 20 mins, or until caps fill with
liquid. Turn over and cook on other side for about 20 mins
or until most liquid has evaporated. Turn mushrooms over
and stuff, with about 1 tsp of stuffing per cap. Mushrooms

www.youtube.com/ilovetocookalot

can be refrigerated covered, for up to one day. Heat for 10 mins (uncovered) in a 375 F oven when ready to serve.

HUMMUS

This fabulous middle eastern dip easy to make at home, and so much better than store bought. You can serve hummus with pita chips, soft or crisped in the oven. It goes great with lamb, or just as a dip with cut up veggies. You can also use it as a sandwich spread. Hummus is a kid friendly dip, with an appealing and nutty taste , while also is thick enough not to be too messy and it is loaded with folate, vitamin B6 and iron!

Ingredients

- 2 large garlic cloves
- ¼ cup water
- Juice of 1-2 lemons
- 1 Tbs olive oil
- ½ tsp salt
- ¼ cup tahini
- 14.5 oz can (drained) chickpeas
- 2 Tbs paprika
- Chopped fresh parsley

Directions

In food processor, place garlic and water, lemon juice and salt and blend to combine. Add chickpeas and olive oil and process until fairly smooth. Add tahini and process again, adding extra water if necessary to thin. Mound in an attractive bowl, sprinkle with paprika and parsley and drizzle with olive oil. Serve at room temperature to appreciate full flavor.

PALMIERS

Savory puff pastry appetizers with mushrooms and parmesan, these delightfully shaped filled slices of puff pastry make a wonderful appetizer. I use a mushroom ragout, bacon and parmesan filling but you could try honey mustard with prosciutto and parm, or sun dried tomatoes with some chopped garlic and parm, or finely chopped anchovy fillets and grated parmesan. You can make these ahead, and freeze unbaked, then bake frozen in a 450 oven for 15 mins.

Ingredients

- 7 oz package puff pastry (or 1/2 of a 1 lb box)
- 5 strips hickory smoked bacon, sautéed and drained and crumbled
- 2 Tbs butter, unsalted
- 8 oz chopped mushrooms - all white, or mixed
- 1/2 tsp salt
- 1/4-1/2 tsp dried wild Spanish thyme
- 1 Tbs half and half or heavy cream
- Freshly ground black pepper to taste
- 2 Tbs parmesan cheese, grated
- 1 egg beaten with 1 Tbs cold water

Directions

Thaw sheet puff pastry at room temperature according to package directions (for about 45 minutes). Preheat oven to 450 F. Melt butter in a heavy skillet and saute mushrooms until they give up their liquid, season with salt and thyme and add half and half and cook over moderate heat until liquid evaporates. Add black pepper roll pastry on lightly

www.youtube.com/ilovetocookalot

floured surface into a 6 in x 14 in rectangle. Spread cooled mushroom mixture over pastry, sprinkle evenly with crumbled bacon and sprinkle evenly with parmesan cheese. Roll up ends (from long side) to meet in the middle. Refrigerate wrapped in plastic, until firm, about 20 mins. Brush with beaten egg on all sides. Cut across into 1/2 inch thick slices and place on a greased baking sheet. Bake until crisp and golden about 10-12 mins. Cool on a wire rack.

PARMESAN CHEESE CRISPS (FRICO)

This recipe is so easy (basically one ingredient!) - and makes a very elegant appetizer or garnish. Be careful with these while they are warm, and try to make this dish on low humidity day for maximum success.

Ingredients

- 1/4 lb high quality parmigiano reggiano
- 1/4 tsp freshly ground black pepper
- optional: add a little cumin or caraway seeds

(these quantities will make about 15 crisps, if you want

more use more cheese)

Directions

Grate cheese on the large holes of a box grater. Sprinkle with black pepper. Prepare a baking pan by lining with parchment paper and spraying lightly with cooking spray. Preheat oven to 400 F. Place level tablespoons of cheese on baking sheet and flatten slightly, with spoon or spatula. Do not crowd as crisps will spread. Bake for about 10 mins or until golden, let cool a few minutes on pan. Carefully transfer to a rack to cool completely.

PARMESAN CHEESE PUFF PASTRY STRAWS

Easy yet so elegant, I like to use this as one of several appetizers at a cocktail party. You can place them in a stemmed glass wrapped with a cloth napkin for a pretty presentation.

Ingredients

- 1 sheet puff pastry, thawed
- 1 egg white, lightly beaten
- 1 tsp Hungarian paprika
- 1/2 cup grated fresh parmigiano reggiano cheese

Directions

Preheat oven to 375 F. Lightly roll puff pastry on a floured board to flatten. Spread egg white over pastry. Sprinkle cheese evenly over pastry and sprinkle with paprika. Using a floured rolling pin gently roll cheese into puff pastry. Cut into long thin strips with a sharp knife, then cut each strip in half horizontally to form 4 inch x 1/2 inch strips. Twist each strip to form a spiral, and place inch apart on a lightly greased or nonstick cooking tray, bake about 8-10 mins or until puffed and golden.

www.youtube.com/ilovetocookalot

PESTO

A classic and so simple to make - much better than store bought. You can use parsley instead of basil if you want, and walnuts instead of pine nuts.

Ingredients

- 2 cups torn fresh basil leaves (discard tough stems)
- 3 Tbs pine nuts
- 1/4 cup freshly grated Parmesan cheese
- 1/2 cup good quality olive oil
- 1 tbs chopped garlic

Directions

Process basil leaves in a food processor, add pine nuts, garlic and cheese and process using on/off pulses. With processor running, stream in olive oil and blend. Store in refrigerator for up to 1 week, or freeze.

Pesto is great on fresh pasta, as a simple sauce or on top of tomato sauce. It makes a great dip also with cut up veggies and it works as a delightful sandwich spread as well with tomato and mozzarella or ham and cheese. Pesto goes well with grilled chicken and you can use it as a rub on a beef before roasting.

PICO DI GALLO

A simple take on a fresh salsa. This is great with chips.

Ingredients

- 3 tomatoes, chopped into very small dice
- 1/2 a red onion chopped into very small dice
- 1/4 cup fresh cilantro finely chopped
- 1 clove garlic, finely chopped
- juice of 1 lime
- 1 Tbs olive oil
- salt
- freshly ground black pepper
- 1/2-1 jalapeno pepper chopped fine

Directions

Combine all ingredients in a pretty bowl. Cover and refrigerate for at least 3 hours for flavors to blend.

PROSCIUTTO WRAPPED FIGS STUFFED WITH MOZZARELLA

Simple, yet elegant preparation of the classic combo - figs and prosciutto.

Ingredients

- 4 fresh black mission figs
- 1 oz fresh mozzarella
- 1/4 tsp ground nutmeg
- 2 oz thin sliced prosciutto, divided into 4 strips
- salt and pepper
- olive oil or cooking spray

Directions

Slice into fig below stem end, but not all the way through just enough to make a pocket. Sprinkle cheese with nutmeg and insert 1/4 oz of cheese into each fig, pushing in and then closing fig back up, tightly. Wrap prosciutto around figs, secure with a toothpick or by threading on a skewer. Brush lightly with olive oil, or spray with cooking spray. Season with salt and pepper. Either grill or broil figs, turning once for about 3 mins per side.

ROAST BEEF SPIRALS

These make a pretty appetizer platter, you can serve with toothpicks if you'd like. Also makes a great lunch wrap style sandwich.

Ingredients

- 2 Flour tortillas (10 inch)
- 2 Tbs soft cheese herb and garlic spread, or creamy horseradish
- 6 oz thinly sliced roast beef
- 1/2 cup baby spinach leaves
- 1 tomato sliced thin
- 1 thin slice red onion

Directions

Spread cheese spread all over one side of each tortilla. Layer spinach leaves on top pressing to adhere. Layer roast beef on bottom third, overlap tomatoes and red onion. Roll up tightly and wrap each in plastic wrap. Chill for at least 30 mins. Cut into 1.5 inch rounds and place on top of lettuce lined platter.

EASY PITA CHIPS

So easy, and very lovely with hummus and or Tzatki.

Ingredients

- Pita bread
- 1 Tbs olive oil
- 1 tsp sea salt
- freshly ground black pepper
- 1 tsp dried herbs de provence
- 1 clove garlic, chopped

Directions

Cut pita into 8 wedges using kitchen shears. Cut along edge of each wedge to make two single layer triangles. Place on a baking sheet, rough side up in a single layer. Combine olive oil, salt, pepper, herbs and garlic. Lightly brush each pita triangle and bake in a 400 F oven for 7 mins. Repeat with additional pita breads to increase number of servings. Remove to wire rack to cool. Store in an air tight container if not serving right away to retain crispness.

www.youtube.com/ilovetocookalot

TORTELLINI SKEWERS

Easy to put together and really colorful on a platter, these antipasti skewers are great warm weather appetizers.

Ingredients

- 1 package cheese tortellini
- 24 small balls fresh mozzarella
- 1 cup fresh basil leaves
- 12 cherry tomatoes, cut in half
- Jar of sundried tomatoes in oil (optional)
- 2 Tbs olive oil
- 1 tsp dried oregano
- Salt and freshly ground black pepper
- 24 skewers or toothpicks

Directions

Cook tortellini according to package directions, drain and rinse in cold water. Toss tortellini, cheese and cherry tomatoes with olive oil, oregano and salt and pepper. Drain sundried tomatoes and cut in half if large. Thread a piece of tortellini, a cherry tomato, a cheese, a basil leaf and a sundried tomato onto each skewer. Arrange on a platter and garnish with fresh basil leaves.

TZATZKI

A simple variation on a classic Greek sauce. Yogurt, dill and cucumber combine with an easy dressing for a refreshing dip for pita triangles or over roasted lamb.

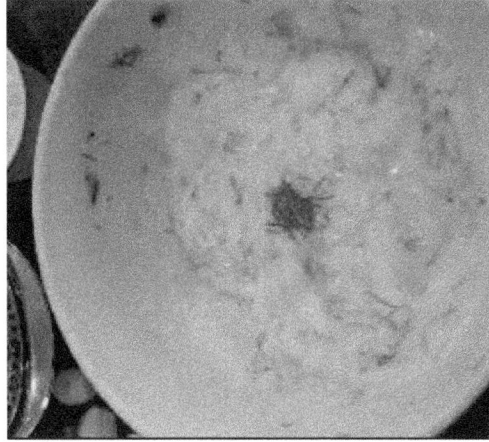

Ingredients

- 1/2 English cucumber, shredded
- 1 Tbs fresh chopped dill
- 1 clove chopped garlic
- juice of 1 lemon
- 1 Tbs white wine vinegar
- 1 Tbs olive oil
- 7 oz Greek drained yogurt
- 1 Tbs shredded white onion
- salt and pepper

Directions

Let shredded cucumber sit in a strainer over a bowl for 1/2 - 4 hours to drain (salt lightly first).
Combine lemon juice, oil, vinegar, dill and salt and pepper.
Whisk to combine, add yogurt, onion and drained cucumber chill for flavors to marry serve at room temp.

www.youtube.com/ilovetocookalot

BREADS

Homemade bread is a wonderful thing - warm from the oven with a fabulous aroma, a freshly baked loaf of bread can make anyone feel loved. A true indulgence is the classic white bread, slathered with butter and paired with all types of food, especially soups. Breads can be simple or fancy. Try the sesame onion bread for a very elegant take on the staff of life. Breads can be fun. Homemade pita breads aren't that complicated and usually will impress your friends and family. Sweet breads, liked spiced pumpkin bread or a nutty banana bread make a great addition to a lazy late morning brunch or serve as a simple breakfast all on their own. Using a standing mixer with a dough hook makes bread making so easy, and you can still add a bit of hand kneading for extra love.

BANANA BREAD

You want the bananas very ripe for this. Great for using up bananas too mushy to eat out of hand.

Ingredients

- 1 cup sugar
- 1/3 cup softened butter
- 2 eggs
- 3-4 mashed very ripe bananas
- 1/2 cup milk
- 1 tsp vanilla
- 1 tsp baking soda
- 1/2 tsp baking powder
- 1/4 tsp salt
- 2 cups all purpose flour (more if needed)
- 1 cup chopped walnuts (optional)

Directions

Cream butter and sugar, add eggs and combine well. Add mashed bananas and milk and vanilla, sift together flour,

www.youtube.com/ilovetocookalot

baking powder, baking soda and salt and add . Stir just to combine, fold in nuts if using. Bake in a loaf pan (grease bottom only) at 350 for 1 hour or until a toothpick inserted in the center comes out clean .Cool for 5 mins in pan, use a knife to loosen edges and turn out onto a rack to cool completely.

BEER BREAD

So easy *and yet very good. I like to change the optional ingredients. In this version I use olives and parmesan, but you could use cheddar cheese and green onions, or sun dried tomatoes and oregano or so many other combinations!*

Ingredients

- 2 2/3 cups self rising flour (or make your own: for each cup of all purpose flour add 1.5 tsp baking powder and .5 tsp salt, sift)
- 12 oz freshly opened beer
- optional: 1 cup coarsely chopped, pitted black olives
- 1/2 cup grated Parmesan cheese
- 1 tsp dried crushed oregano

Directions

Use cooking spray on a loaf pan (9x5x3).
Preheat oven to 350 F. Combine flour with olives, Parmesan cheese and oregano if desired. Add beer and gently fold in to combine, spoon in to loaf pan. Bake for 55 mins, or until a toothpick inserted in center comes out clean. Cool on a wire rack for 5 mins, then turn out and continue to cool.

www.youtube.com/ilovetocookalot

BUTTERMILK SKILLET CORN BREAD

Easy and wonderful paired with Chili.

Ingredients

- 3/4 cup stoneground corn meal
- 1 cup all purpose bread flour (unbleached)
- 1 tsp baking powder
- 1/4 tsp baking soda
- 1 tsp salt
- 1/4 cup sugar
- 1/4 cup oil
- 1 egg, beaten
- 1 cup buttermilk
- 2 Tbs butter

Directions

Combine dry ingredients, sifting together if lumpy. Beat egg and add oil and buttermilk add to dry ingredients. Melt butter in cast iron pan and when bubbling add batter. Place on middle rack in oven and bake 20-25 mins until done. Cool for 5 mins on wire rack and slice into wedges serve warm.

IRISH SODA BREAD

This simple take on this classic bread is delicious, great in the morning with butter and jam – or all by itself.

Ingredients

- 4 cups flour
- 1/4 cup sugar
- 1 Tbs baking powder
- 1 tsp baking soda
- 1/4 tsp salt
- 1/2 cup unsalted butter, softened
- 1 cup buttermilk
- 1 egg
- 1/2 cup raisins plumped in 1/2 cup hot water and drained

for wash:

- 1/4 cup melted butter
- 1/4 cup buttermilk

Directions

Combine dry ingredients, add butter and cut in, add 1 cup buttermilk and egg and mix to combine. Stir in raisins. Gather dough into a ball and shape into a loaf and place on a greased baking pan. Using a sharp knife, cut an X into top of dough. Baste with a mixture of wash ingredients prior to baking in a preheated 375 F oven and then baste every 20 mins or so. Bake for 40-50 mins or until loaf is browned, bottom is browned and a toothpick inserted into center comes out clean. Cool on a wire rack.

ONION SESAME BREAD

This bread is gorgeous and super delicious as well. It also freezes very well, just slice it and wrap in plastic.

Ingredients

Filling:

- 1/4 cup butter
- 1 vidalia onion, chopped
- 1 clove garlic, chopped
- 1.5 Tbs grated parmesan cheese
- 1 Tbs raw sesame seeds
- salt
- 1/2 tsp paprika

Bread:

- 1/4 cup sugar
- 1 package active dry yeast
- 1/4 cup warm water to proof yeast
- 1 egg
- salt
- 1/2 cup butter at room temp
- 1/2 cup whole milk
- 1/2 cup hot water
- 4-5 cups bread flour

www.youtube.com/ilovetocookalot

Directions

Prepare filling:
melt butter in a cast iron skillet and saute onions until soft. Add garlic and saute another 2 mins. Add parmesan, sesame seeds and salt and paprika. Remove from skillet and refrigerate until cold.

Prepare dough:
in a small bowl dissolve yeast in 1/4 cup hot water and add a little (1 Tbs) of the sugar to proof.

In the bowl of a standing mixer combine remaining ingredients (only use 4 cups of the flour) Using the dough hook, stir on low setting to combine ingredients. Add yeast once it has foamed into a bubbly liquid. Increase speed to knead dough for several minutes, adding additional flour as necessary. When dough forms a ball, remove from machine and knead by hand on a floured surface until dough is smooth and elastic. Gather into a ball and place in a greased bowl to rise about 1 hour, or until doubled in bulk. Punch dough down and divide in half. Roll each half into a 8x13 inch rectangle and spread 1/2 of filling on each rectangle. Cut each rectangle into three equal strips lengthwise and roll up each strip to encase filling. Braid three strips together for each loaf. Let rise on greased baking sheets for about 1 hour. Bake in a preheated 350 oven for 30-40 minutes, until golden. Cool on wire racks.

www.youtube.com/ilovetocookalot

PITA BREAD

Making pita bread at home impresses everyone, and its really quite easy.

Ingredients

- 1 cup warm water
- 1 package active dry yeast (about 2 tsps)
- 1 Tbs sugar
- 2 Tbs olive oil
- 1 tsp sea salt
- 2.5 cups all purpose unbleached flour

Directions

Combine yeast, water and sugar in a warmed bowl. Allow to proof 5 mins. Add salt, olive oil and 1 cup flour and stir with dough hook on a standing mixer (or by hand), add 1.5 cups additional flour (a little more if needed) and stir with dough hook or by hand until dough forms a ball and comes away from sides of bowl. Continue to knead 5 mins more. Let dough rest for 20 mins, covered Cut dough into 8 pieces and roll each into a ball. Cover dough with towel Preheat oven to 500 F, working with one piece at a time roll each piece of dough out into a very thin circle (1/8" thick). Place on a piece of foil and place in oven on center rack, bake 5-8 mins or until puffed and browned. Remove from oven and wrap loosly in foil, repeat until all pitas are made.

www.youtube.com/ilovetocookalot

SPICED PUMPKIN BREAD

Wonderful bread to celebrate the fall, this makes a lovely addition to Sunday morning brunches.

Ingredients

- 3 cups sugar
- 1 cup canola oil
- 3 eggs
- 1 15 oz can pure pumpkin
- 3 cups flour, sifted with
- 1 tsp each cloves, cinnamon and nutmeg
- 1 tsp baking soda
- 1/2 tsp baking powder
- 1/2 tsp salt

Directions

Combine sugar and oil. Beat in eggs and pumpkin, add sifted dry ingredients in two batches stirring to combine pour into two buttered loaf pans (or use cooking spray). Bake at 350 for about 1 hour or until tester comes out clean, cool on wire rack.

WHITE BREAD

Comfort food at its best!

Ingredients

- 2.5 cups warm water, divided
- 1 package active dry yeast
- 1 Tbs sugar
- 6-7 cups all purpose bread flour, divided
- 1/2 tsp salt
- 1/3 cup softened butter

Directions

Rinse mixer bowl with hot water. Add 1 cup warm (110 F) water to bowl, add yeast and sugar Let sit for 5 mins until bubbly. Add 3 cups flour and salt to bowl and mix on low with a dough hook. Add 3-4 cups additional flour and mix on medium until dough forms a ball. Continue to knead with mixer for 10 mins, or knead by hand. Add butter, 1 Tbs at a time and mix dough will come apart at first but will reform into a ball. Turn dough out onto a lightly floured surface, knead briefly and form into a ball. Place in a large bowl which you have greased lightly, cover and let rise until doubled in bulk, about 45 mins. Punch dough down, divide in half and roll each half into a rectangle. Fold dough over in thirds and pinch edges together to form a loaf, repeat with other half. Place each loaf in a greased bread pan, cover and let rise until doubled in bulk, about 45 mins. Bake in a 375 F oven for 25-30 mins or until golden honey brown, and remove from loaf pans and cool on a wire rack.

www.youtube.com/ilovetocookalot

SALADS

Salads can be attractive and healthy additions to any meal –They can be starters, or served as the main event. Fruit salads can also make wonderful desserts. When I think of salads I think of all kinds of combinations of fruit and vegetables and sometimes cheese. I don't unusually think of greens, I'd rather get my leafy greens from vegetables. Salads can make a light meal or a wonderful addition to a picnic or BBQ. Try the wild rice salad at your next picnic. Sometimes salads can be desserts - the mixed berry mango salad paired with a little creme fraiche makes a lovely ending to a robust meal. The goat cheese salad is an elegant start for any meal.

ARTICHOKE AND ASPARAGUS SALAD

Very elegant salad makes a wonderful start to a formal meal.

Ingredients

- 1 bunch asparagus
- 1 14.5 oz can artichoke hearts, packed in water
- 1 cup cherry tomatoes, cut in half
- 10 green olives with pimentos, sliced
- Lettuce leaves

Dressing:

- zest from one lemon, grated
- juice of 1/2 lemon
- 2 Tbs olive oil
- 2 Tbs dijon mustard
- salt
- freshly ground black pepper

Directions

Snap asparagus spears into 1.5 inch lengths, discarding tough ends steam asparagus over water or chicken broth for 3-5 mins until crisp tender. Drain and place in a bowl of cold water to stop cooking. Combine tomatoes and coarsely chopped drained artichoke hearts, drain asparagus and add to bowl. Add sliced olives. Combine all dressing ingredients and shake or stir. Plate up by placing a few lettuce leaves on each plate and then dividing salad atop them. Drizzle with dressing and add some freshly ground black pepper if desired.

ARUGULA, BACON AND APPLE SALAD

Simple, fast and interesting - really yummy salad.

Ingredients

- 1 lb baby arugula, torn
- 1 granny smith apple, thinly sliced
- 5 slices bacon, cooked and crumbled (fat drained and reserved)
- 1/4 cup chopped walnuts (toasted if desired)
- 1-2 oz aged white cheddar, shredded

Dressing:

- juice of 1 lemon
- 2 Tbs cider vinegar
- 2 tsp dijon mustard
- 1 shallot, finely chopped
- 1 tsp sugar (optional)
- 1/2 tsp salt
- 1 Tbs bacon fat
- 1 Tbs olive oil
- freshly ground black pepper

Directions

Combine salad ingredients. Stir together all dressing ingredients except fat and oil. Whisk in fat and oil briskly. Pour dressing over salad and toss gently but thoroughly.

www.youtube.com/ilovetocookalot

BLACK BEAN AND PEPPER SALAD

This colorful salad plates up beautifully and pairs very well with grilled fish or meats.

Ingredients

- 1 can black beans, rinsed and drained
- 1/2 cup diced red onion (small 1/2" dice)
- 1/2 cup cooked corn kernels
- 1 diced red bell pepper
- 1 diced yellow bell pepper
- 3 Tbs chopped fresh parsley
- 1 clove minced garlic
- 3 Tbs red wine vinegar
- 1/4-1/2 cup olive oil
- salt and pepper

Directions

Combine beans, onion, peppers, parsley, corn and garlic whisk together oil and vinegar add salt and pepper and pour over salad and toss gently.

www.youtube.com/ilovetocookalot

CAPRESE SALAD

This classic combination of tomatoes, mozzarella and basil works best with truly good tomatoes. You can also do a version on skewers using cherry tomatoes.

Ingredients

- 3-4 ripe tomatoes
- 15 fresh basil leaves
- fresh mozzarella
- extra virgin olive oil
- coarse sea salt, black pepper

Directions

Thinly slice tomatoes. Slice mozzarella, cut basil leaves in half if large. Artfully arrange tomato, cheese and basil slightly overlapping in a circle pattern on a pretty serving platter. Drizzle with olive oil and sprinkle with sea salt and freshly ground black pepper.

www.youtube.com/ilovetocookalot

CHICKPEA SALAD

This Mediterranean inspired recipe is very flexible. Chickpeas marry beautifully with lemon juice, freshly ground pepper and a little high quality olive oil. Optional additions can render this almost a meal in itself.

Ingredients

- 1 can chickpeas (preferably without preservatives)
- Juice from 1 lemon
- 1 clove garlic, minced
- 4 Tbs white onion, chopped
- 1/2 english cucumber, diced
- 3-4 tomatoes, diced
- 2 radishes finely sliced
- 1 Tbs extra virgin olive oil
- 1 tsp sea salt
- 1 tsp freshly ground black pepper (or more)

To serve:

- shavings of fresh parmesan cheese
- baby greens
- optional add ins: 1/4 cup chopped fresh parsley
- 1/4 cup diced fresh mozzarella

www.youtube.com/ilovetocookalot

Directions

Drain and rinse chickpeas, combine in a large bowl with all
other ingredients, chill
well. Serve on a bed of greens (wild baby greens, rocket or
baby spinach).

CORN AND LIME SALAD

Easy and refreshing summer salad.

Ingredients

- Juice of 1 lime
- 5 red radishes, sliced thinly and then quartered
- 1 lb frozen baby yellow and white corn
- 1 Tbs sugar
- 1 Tbs olive oil
- salt and freshly ground black pepper

Directions

Blanch corn in boiling salted water for 2 mins. Drain. In a pretty serving bowl combine lime juice, oil, sugar, salt and pepper. Add corn and radishes, toss to coat. Serve at room temperature or chill.

CUCUMBER SALAD

Easy and refreshing Asian inspired salad.

Ingredients

- 1 English cucumber ("seedless")
- 2 Tbs rice wine vinegar
- ½ red onion
- 1 tsp sesame oil
- Salt and pepper

Directions

Using a mandolin, very thinly slice cucumber into paper thin rounds. Thinly slice onion as well, combine rice wine vinegar and a dash of sesame oil in a pretty bowl, add cucumber and onion. Toss to coat. Season with salt and pepper.

COLD NOODLE SALAD

Easy Asian inspired noodle salad - great for picnics and BBQ's.

Ingredients

- 12 oz Soba Noodles
- large pot of water
- 1/3 cup soy sauce (low sodium)
- 1/3 cup brown rice vinegar
- 1 tsp toasted sesame oil
- 1 clove garlic, minced
- finely chopped or shredded carrots
- juice of 1 lime, and zest from 1 lime
- 1 tsp sugar (white or brown)
- 1/2 tsp crushed red pepper

Directions

Cook noodles according to package directions (about 5 mins, drain and rinse in cold water).
Combine all dressing ingredients with a whisk, add noodles and toss. Serve at room temperature or cold. Garnish with 2 tbs chopped roasted peanuts and fresh chopped cilantro or green onion if desired.

www.youtube.com/ilovetocookalot

GOAT CHEESE SALAD

Super easy yet elegant starter, a simple bed of greens topped with warm breaded goat cheese, dried cranberries and walnuts.

Ingredients

- 4 oz plain goat cheese log
- 1/4 cup flour
- salt, pepper
- 1/2 cup Italian seasoned bread crumbs
- 1 egg beaten with 1 Tbs water
- 16 oz wild baby greens mix
- 1/2 cup dried cranberries
- 1/2 cup chopped walnuts
- 2 Tbs aged balsamic vinegar
- 1 Tbs olive oil
- 8 cherry tomatoes, quartered

Directions

Cut goat cheese log into 4 slices, shape into rounds, dredge in flour, egg, and breadcrumbs
refrigerate at least 1 hour. Heat olive oil and sauté goat

www.youtube.com/ilovetocookalot

cheese rounds till golden brown on each side. Divide baby greens onto four plates, sprinkle each plate with dried cranberries, chopped walnuts. Drizzle a little vinegar and oil over each, top with one warm goat cheese round each and decorate with cherry tomatoes.

JELLO FRUIT MOLD

Really pretty molded fruit salad, great for the 4th of July or Memorial day.

Ingredients

- 4 cups white cranberry juice
- 1/2 cup sugar
- 2 envelopes unflavored gelatin
- 2 cups cut up strawberries
- 2 cups blueberries
- Whipped cream

Directions

Soften gelatin in 1/2 cup juice, then heat remaining juice and sugar to boiling, remove from heat and stir in softened gelatin until completely dissolved. Spray an **8 cup fancy mold** with cooking spray, place 2 cups of strawberries evenly in the bottom and pour over 2 cups of the gelatin mixture. Let set in the refrigerator for ½ hour. Add 2 cups of blueberries to the remaining gelatin mixture and gently spoon that on top of the semi-set strawberry layer. Chill the mold, covered with plastic wrap, overnight. Dip the mold in hot water to loosen and unmold onto a pretty plate. Serve with whipped cream if desired.

JICAMA AND ORANGE SALAD

Really Easy and Refreshing Summer salad with Jicama, Orange and honey dressing.

Ingredients

- 1 medium jicama, peeled and cut into matchstick slices
- 1 cup baby carrots cut into matchstick slices
- 2 medium navel oranges, peeled and cut into chunks

Dressing:

- 2 Tbs orange juice
- juice of 1/2-1 lime
- 1/2 Tbs olive oil
- 1 Tbs clover honey
- pinch of salt
- 10 mint leaves, sliced into thin strips

Directions

Combine jicama, carrots and orange, whisk dressing ingredients in a small bowl and pour over salad toss to coat. Garnish with fresh mint if desired. Let refrigerate for several hours to blend flavor.

www.youtube.com/ilovetocookalot

CLASSIC MACARONI SALAD

A lightened version of a summer time favorite. Macaroni salad with bell pepper and celery for crunch and sour cream for richness.

Ingredients

- 1/2-1 lb elbow macaroni (if you use the larger amount you might need a bit more dressing)
- 1/2 bell pepper, diced
- 1.5 Tbs shredded white onion
- 1.5 Tbs sweet relish
- 1 Tbs low fat milk
- 1 Tbs low fat sour cream
- 1/4 cup light mayonnaise
- 2 stalks celery diced
- 1/2 carrot shredded
- salt and pepper

Directions

Cook pasta according to package directions, drain and let cool combine all dressing ingredients, add pasta and stir to coat let refrigerate for 1 hour to allow flavors to blend.

www.youtube.com/ilovetocookalot

MANGO BERRY SALAD WITH GINGER

Easy and quick to put together. This summer dessert salad is fabulous and if you have a ripe mango out of this world!

Ingredients

- 1 cup water
- 1/3 cup white sugar
- 1 Tbs peeled fresh ginger sliced
- 3 Tbs chopped fresh mint
- 1 mango, peeled and cut into bite size chunks (about 2 cups)
- 1 cup blueberries
- 1 cup strawberries, cut up

Directions

Heat water and sugar to dissolve sugar, add ginger bring to a boil, lower heat and let simmer 5 mins. Remove from heat and add mint. Let steep until cool. Strain mixture through a fine sieve and press down on solids to get flavor out. Discard solids. Combine mango and berries in a pretty bowl and pour sauce over Garnish with fresh mint if desired.

MILLET SALAD

Healthy and whole grain this salad pairs well with roasted meats.

Ingredients

- 1 cup millet
- 1 Tbs olive oil (optional)
- 2 1/4 cups water
- 4 radishes, thinly sliced into half moons then cut in half again
- 1/2 English cucumber cut into small dice
- 2 Tbs chopped black olives
- 3 Tbs chopped Italian parsley
- 2 Tbs olive oil
- 1.5 Tbs red wine vinegar
- 1 tsp salt black pepper

Directions

Heat a cast iron skillet over medium heat, add olive oil if using, rinse and drain millet
Add to skillet and toast stirring frequently for 7 mins or until a deep golden brown. Add water and bring to a low boil, cover and lower heat cook for 20 mins undisturbed. Combine olive oil, vinegar and salt in a bowl, whisk well. Add veggies, black pepper and millet. Toss to combine. Let stand at room temp at least 10 mins before serving.

www.youtube.com/ilovetocookalot

PASTA SALAD WITH TRI-COLOR ROASTED PEPPERS

A really colorful pretty salad.

Ingredients

- 3 bell peppers (yellow, red and orange)
- 1 clove minced garlic
- 2 anchovies, packed in olive oil
- 3 Tbs olive oil
- freshly ground black pepper
- 1 tsp sea salt
- 4 oz cubed whole milk mozzarella
- 8 leaves fresh basil
- 1 Tbs capers, packed in brine
- 1 lb cooked spiral shaped pasta or penne rinsed and drained

Directions

Prick peppers with fork all over and bake on foil lined sheet for 20-40 mins at 450 F, turning periodically remove from oven and place in a paper bag for 5-10 mins, seed and peel and chop peppers. Cook pasta for 8-10 mins . Mince garlic with anchovies, add pasta, olive oil, salt and pepper. Add roasted peppers and stir in basil and cheese and capers. Toss to coat. Serve at room temp.

POTATO SALAD – GERMAN STYLE

Bacon and apple cider vinegar make this classic dish wonderful to eat.

Ingredients

- 2.5 lbs red skinned potatoes
- 1/2 lb bacon
- 1 onion, finely chopped
- 2 stalks celery, chopped
- 1/2 green bell pepper, chopped
- 6 Tbs apple cider vinegar
- 3 Tbs sugar
- 1 Tbs paprika
- salt and pepper

Directions

Cook potatoes with skins on in boiling salted water to cover until tender but not mushy. Drain, cool a little and chop into 1" chunks. Peel first if you want. Saute bacon, drain on paper towels and crumble into small pieces. Pour off all but 2 Tbs bacon fat, in remaining hot fat saute onion, celery and bell pepper until onion is soft. Add vinegar, sugar, paprika and salt and pepper. Cook and stir briefly, return bacon to pan. Pour dressing over potatoes in a pretty bowl and toss gently to coat. Serve warm or at room temperature.

www.youtube.com/ilovetocookalot

SHRIMP, VEGGIE AND NOODLE DINNER SALAD

One bowl dinner. Great use for ramen noodles.

Ingredients

Dressing:

- 1/3 cup olive oil
- 1/4 cup lime juice
- 1 tsp lime zest, grated
- 2 Tbs chopped fresh mint
- 1 tsp chopped fresh peeled ginger
- 1 tsp sugar

Salad:

- 1 lb deveined, peeled cooked shrimp cut in half if large
- 8 oz snow peas, destringed and cut in half
- 8 radishes, cut into eighths
- 1/3 cup chopped green onions
- 7 oz ramen type noodles, discard seasoning packet
- 1 can baby corn, drained and cut in half

Directions

Whisk together dressing ingredients and add baby corns, let sit for 30 mins. Cook ramen noodles briefly, according to package directions, breaking up into small pieces. Add salad ingredients and toss to coat.

www.youtube.com/ilovetocookalot

TROPICAL FRUIT SALAD

A simple but lovely combination of tropical fruits this salad goes great with a wide variety of grilled meats or fish. Also lovely when paired with Brazilian black bean stew.

Ingredients

- 1 mango, peeled and flesh diced (a mango has a long flat pit in the center)
- 1 kiwi, peeled and diced
- 1/2 pineapple, peeled, cored and diced
- 1 ripe banana, peeled and diced
- optional: 1/2 ripe papaya, peeled, seeded and diced
- optional: 1 Tbs lime or lemon juice
- garnish: sliced star fruit

Directions

Cut fruit into small dice (1/4-1/2"). Combine all ingredients, but add banana right before serving or it will discolor. Add 1 Tbs lemon or lime juice if desired.

PINEAPPLE BOAT FRUIT SALAD

Really pretty way to serve a fruit salad.

Ingredients

- 1 large pineapple, carefully cut in half and flesh scooped out, diced, core discarded
- 1 pint raspberries
- 2 cups blue berries
- 2 kiwis, peeled and sliced into 1/4 inch rings, then quartered
- 2 mangos (ripe please, or don't use -I went through 4 to get 2) diced
- 1/4 watermelon diced
- 1 can mandarin oranges packed in juice if you can find them and drained
- 1 lb strawberries, diced
- mint, chopped fine and clusters of leaves for garnish

Directions

Combine all fruit in a large bowl and toss gently to coat, add chopped mint. Scoop into pineapple boats (or use a bowl) and garnish with fresh mint sprigs.

www.youtube.com/ilovetocookalot

ROASTED VEGGIE TRI COLORED SALAD

Beautiful salad, featuring brilliant reds, golds and greens. Easy and fabulous and oh so pretty!

Ingredients

salad:

- 1 bunch red beets, about 3-4 medium, with tops
- 1 bunch golden beets
- 1 lb thin asparagus
- 1 Tbs olive oil
- 1 tsp sea salt
- 1 head garlic

dressing:

- 1/4 cup olive oil
- 1/4 cup fresh orange juice
- 1 Tbs dried minced onion
- 2 Tbs balsamic vinegar
- salt and pepper

www.youtube.com/ilovetocookalot

Directions

Wash beets, and trim tops to 1" above beet top. Roast beets, colors separately, wrapped in aluminum foil loosely but completely add garlic cloves, unpeeled to beets, and roast 1 hour.
Snap ends off asparagus and place on a baking sheet, roll in 1 Tbs olive oil to coat
sprinkle with 1 tsp salt. Roast in 450F oven for 10-12 mins. Combine soft roasted garlic (no skins) and mash with 1/4 cup olive oil, balsamic vinegar, orange juice, onion and salt and pepper. whisk to blend Slice and dice beets, keep colors separate, combine each veggie with 2 tbs dressing and marinate. Plate up together.

SPINACH SALAD

Wilted spinach greens with bacon . A classic and wonderful salad.

Ingredients

- 1 lb baby spinach
- 5 pieces smoked bacon
- ½ red onion, chopped
- 2 Tbs flour
- 1 Tbs sugar
- 1/3 cup apple cider vinegar
- optional: 1 hard boiled egg

Directions

Cook bacon and drain on paper towels. Let cool and chop coarsely. Add flour to hot bacon fat and stir over medium heat, add sugar and red onion. Add apple cider vinegar. Plate spinach on individual plates or on one big pretty platter. Pour warm dressing over spinach and toss to coat greens and wilt them. Sprinkle bacon pieces over salad, add quartered peeled egg if desired.

THREE BEAN SALAD

Classic, fun summer salad. Make it ahead and take it on a picnic.

Ingredients

- 12 oz cleaned snapped green beans
- 12 oz cleaned snapped wax beans
- 14 oz can kidney beans
- 1 Tbs olive oil
- 1/4 cup red wine vinegar
- freshly ground blk pepper
- 1 tsp salt
- 1/2 tsp honey or sugar
- 1/2 tsp dried oregano
- 2 Tbs chopped fresh parsley
- 2 Tbs chopped red onion

Directions

Cook green and wax beans over boiling water for 5 mins. Combine oil, vinegar and spices, salt and pepper and honey. Add drained beans. Drain and rinse kidney beans and add to salad. Add parsley and onion and toss to coat. Serve warm, chilled or at room temp.

www.youtube.com/ilovetocookalot

WALDORF SALAD

A classic salad, lightened up just a bit by mixing low fat yogurt with mayo. You could use green grapes or raisins in place of the currents, or just leave them out altogether.

Ingredients

- 2-3 eating apples (such as red delicious or Jona gold) cut into 1/2 inch chunks
- 2 stalks celery diced
- 2 Tbs walnuts coarsely chopped
- 2 Tbs currents, plumped in hot water for 10 mins and then drained
- 1 Tbs lemon juice
- 2 Tbs low fat plain yogurt
- 2 Tbs mayonnaise
- green leaf lettuce, optional

Directions

Combine apples with lemon juice and toss to coat. Add celery, walnuts and currents. Add yogurt and mayo and gently blend to coat salad with dressing. Serve on a bed of lettuce, if desired.

www.youtube.com/ilovetocookalot

WATERMELON SALAD

A simple refreshing salad combining the sweetness of watermelon and mint with the sharpness of arugula and feta and basil.

Ingredients

- 5 cups seedless watermelon cubed into 0.5 inch dice
- 1/2 cup thinly sliced red onion
- 1/4 cup thinly sliced fresh mint
- 1/4 cup thinly sliced fresh basil
- 1 cup feta cheese crumbles
- 1 tsp sea salt
- 7 oz baby arugula
- 3 Tbs fresh lemon juice
- black pepper, optional

Directions

Combine all ingredients in a pretty serving bowl and toss.

WILD RICE SALAD

A really simple but delicious wild rice salad. Perfect for a picnic.

Ingredients

- 1 cup cooked wild rice, or brown rice
- 1 tsp lemon juice
- 2 Tbs chopped parsley
- 1/4 cup chopped green onion
- 1/2 cup finely chopped celery
- 1/2 cup chopped cooked brocollini or broccoli
- 2 tbs red wine vinegar
- 1 Tbs dijon mustard
- 1 Tbs olive oil
- salt and freshly ground black pepper

Directions

Combine rice, lemon juice, parsley, green onion and celery and brocollini whisk together vinegar, dijon mustard and olive oil and pour over rice mixture, toss to coat. Season with salt and pepper , chill for up to 8 hours.

SOUPS

Soup can serve as a whole meal or an elegant starter. Lovely in cold weather, a robust stew conjures images of comfort and warmth. Cold soups are delightful in summer and can be served as desserts if fruit based, or first courses if vegetable based. For starters I often go with oyster pan roast, mushroom soup or asparagus soup. Pair a bowl of soup with a loaf of bread; add a salad and it's a meal. Wedding soup is an all-time favorite with my family , and a hearty bowl of minestrone or a meat based stew is always a delight to come home to. Another great thing about soups and stews is the make ahead factor. So go ahead and make a big pot of wonderful flavorful soup to share!

ASPARAGUS SOUP

Elegant starter, very pretty plated and absolutely delicious.

Ingredients

- 4.5 - 5.5 cups low sodium chicken broth
- 1/4 tsp saffron threads
- 1/3 cup shelled natural pine nuts
- 3.5 lbs asparagus
- 1 large russet potato
- 1/2 stick butter
- 1/2 cup chopped flat leaf parsley
- salt and pepper to taste

Directions

Bring 1/2 cup broth to a boil Remove from heat and add saffron. Let steep 15 minutes. Toast pine nuts in a dry heavy skillet (watch carefully they burn easily) chop nuts. Trim asparagus into 2" pieces, reserve tips. Blanch tips in boiling salted water 2 mins, plunge into cold water to arrest cooking and drain, dry and set aside. Dice peeled potato into 1/2 inch cubes. Cook remaining asparagus pieces in melted butter in soup pot, stir for 3 minutes. Add potato cubes, saffron broth and 4 cups broth and simmer for 20-40 minutes (depending on how thick asparagus is, until tender). Puree mixture in batches in a blender (careful of hot liquids) Return to soup pot, add additional broth until

www.youtube.com/ilovetocookalot

desired consistency is reached, add 1/2 of reserved asparagus tips and cook on low heat until heated through.

Ladle soup into bowls, top with chopped parsley, pinenuts and asparagus tips.

AVOCADO SOUP

Super easy soup to serve cold, great for outdoor summer dining.

Ingredients

- 1 ripe avocado
- ½ seedless cucumber, diced
- 2 Tbs low fat sour cream
- 11/2 cups chicken or vegetable broth
- 1/2 tsp salt
- Juice of 1 lime
- Chopped radish
- Chopped parsley
- freshly ground black pepper

Directions

1 ripe avocado Combine cucumber and avocado (remove from peel and remove pit, cut into chunks) with sour cream and lime juice in a blender. Puree until smooth, add broth. Add additional chopped avocado and cucumber to soup for texture, if desired. Refrigerate for at least 1 hour and up to 8 hours. Serve garnished with radish, parsley and black pepper.

MINESTRONE

A take on winter minestrone, very hearty yet meatless. Use vegetable broth to make it completely vegetarian, or add some cooked sausage chunks to make it even heartier.

Ingredients

- 1 onion chopped
- 1 cup chopped carrots
- 1 cup chopped celery
- 2 cloves chopped garlic
- 2 Tbs olive oil
- 1 14.5 oz can crushed tomatoes
- Rind from parmesan cheese
- 8 cups chicken broth
- 1 can cannelloni beans, rinsed and drained
- 1 lb fresh baby spinach
- ½ cup ditalini pasta (little tubes)
- ½ cup chopped fresh flat leaf parsley
- ¼ cup chopped fresh basil
- 1 zucchini, cut into half-moon chunks
- 1 summer squash, cut into half-moon chunks
- Optional: fresh pesto

Directions

In a large heavy soup put heat olive oil and add onion, celery, carrots and garlic. Cook over medium flame to soften vegetables. Add chicken stock, tomatoes and parmesan rind. Add some freshly grated pepper and bring to a boil. Add pasta and lower heat to medium, cook 8 mins. Add spinach, beans and fresh herbs. Simmer over low heat another 10 mins. Serve garnished with a tbs of fresh pesto if desired.

CREAM OF CELERY SOUP

A very elegant and quite healthy soup.

Ingredients

- 2 Tbs unsalted butter
- 1 Tbs olive oil
- 1 bunch celery, stems and leaves, chopped (about 5 cups)
- 1 cup vidalla onion, chopped
- 1/4 cup chopped green onion
- 2 russet potatoes, peeled and diced
- 6 cups chicken or vegetable broth
- 1/2 tsp celery salt
- 1/2 tsp celery seed
- freshly ground black pepper

Directions

Melt butter and oil in soup pot. Add vegetables and saute for about 15 mins. Add broth, spices, bring to a boil and lower heat to a simmer. Simmer for about 35 mins. Strain, reserving soup broth. Puree solids with a little broth in

www.youtube.com/ilovetocookalot

blender in batches until smooth. Return to soup pot. Combine soup broth with puree until desired consistency is reached. Heat through. Garnish with celery leaves, or parsley or chopped green onion.

LIONS HEAD SOUP

Asian flavored meatballs nestled in cabbage form lion heads and manes, a delicious dish.

Ingredients

For meatballs:

- 1.5 lbs coarsely ground pork butt
- 2 tsp fresh peeled ginger, finely chopped
- 1 scallion finely chopped
- 2 tsp coarse sea salt
- 2 tsp rice wine
- 2 tsp toasted sesame oil
- 1 egg white
- white pepper, or black pepper to taste

for stir-fry:

www.youtube.com/ilovetocookalot

- 1 large Chinese cabbage, reserve 3 large leaves shred the remaining leaves into wide long strips,
- core chopped coarsely (keep core and leaves separate)
- 3 Tbs canola oil
- salt and pepper
- 1/4 cup rice wine

meatball glaze:

- 1 Tbs beef stock
- 1 Tbs cornstarch
- 1 Tbs soy sauce
- 2.75 cups beef stock

Directions

Combine all seasonings and egg white for meatballs, add meat and stir with hands. Throw into sides of bowl to blend. Set aside. Heat wok over medium high heat, add 3 Tbs vegetable oil and swirl to coat. Add thick cabbage core pieces, and stirfry one minute, add cabbage leaves and stirfry 1 min more season with salt and pepper and add rice wine, stirfry 30 more seconds. Remove cabbage to a large soup pot. Add stock. Combine all ingredients for glaze in a small bowl. Heat 1 Tbs oil in a large cast iron skillet Form meatballs using 2 Tbs of meat, glaze each meatball in glaze and panfry till golden on all sides. Place meatballs on top of cabbage cover with reserved three leaves and bring to a boil, cover pot and reduce heat to a low simmer and cook for 1 hour. Serve a little cabbage with a meatball and some stock.

MUSHROOM SOUP

Simple, delicious mushroom soup - use any combination of wild and cultivated mushrooms. Easy, fast and oh so good!

Ingredients

- 2 cups chopped onion
- 3 Tbs butter
- cooking soray
- 6 oz crimini mushrooms, cleaned and chopped
- 6 oz shitake mushrooms, cleaned and chopped
- 10 oz white mushrooms, cleaned and chopped
- 1 Tbs chopped fresh thyme
- 2 Tbs flour
- 5 cups beef broth
- optional: 3 Tbs brandy

Directions

Coat pot with cooking spray, melt butter. Add all mushrooms and saute until juices are released, about 8 mins. Add brandy, if using, cook 30 secs. Add flour and stir and cook 1 minute longer. Slowly add broth and bring to a boil. Lower heat and simmer 10 minutes. Add salt and freshly ground black pepper to taste. Puree in batches in a blender, return to pot and heat through. Optionally, add 1/2 cup heavy cream for additional richness.

OYSTER PAN ROAST

Fabulous rich little dish - perfect as the prelude to a romantic dinner - easy and impressive! Oysters are, arguably, the most famous of all aphrodisiacs. Venus/Aphrodite sprang of course from an oyster shell - Goddess of Sea and Love!

Ingredients

- 16 oysters, shucked, with 1/2 cup of their liquor
- 2 Tbs ketchup style chili sauce
- 2 Tbs dry white wine
- 2 tsp Worcestershire sauce
- 1/2 tsp celery salt
- 1/2 stick (4 Tbs) unsalted butter
- 1/2 cup heavy cream
- 2 slices crusty bread, toasted
- 1 tsp paprika

Directions

Heat a double boiler over simmering water; remember water should not touch bottom of upper pot. Stir in oysters, their liquor, chili sauce, wine, worcestershire, celery salt and 2 Tbs of the butter. Cook about 5 minutes until oysters edges curl. Add cream and bring to a simmer - do not boil! Butter toasts and divide stew into two bowls, top with toasts and a little paprika.

You could follow this with something classic and simple, say Steak Diane and asparagus and silky smooth mashed potatoes - or something more complicated, like individual

www.youtube.com/ilovetocookalot

beef wellingtons - or just do multiple appetizers - a seared fois gras, some canapes maybe some shrimp?

NOTE: you should shuck oysters just before using. It's not hard - you can use a screw driver and a thick kitchen towel or, they actually sell little oyster shucker knives! Just make sure to put the knife or flat head of the screwdriver into the hinge of the oyster, hold it pointing away from you wrap hand in towel and twist the blade, do this over a bowl to catch the oyster juice. You could also have your fishmonger do this for you ahead of time - the same day - but don't buy oysters in a jar for this dish!

SPLIT PEA SOUP

Wonderful in winter or fall this hearty soup can go completely vegetarian if you desire, just use vegetable stock or even water and skip the ham.

Ingredients

- 1 Tbs butter
- 1 chopped onion
- 3 stalks celery
- 3 large carrots
- 1 lb split green peas (dried)
- 2 cups water
- 2 qts additional liquid (chicken stock, vegetable stock or water)
- salt and pepper
- 1 tsp garlic powder
- 1 bay leaf, optional
- 6 oz ham steak, cubed or 1 smoked ham hock or leftover ham bone

Directions

Wash, drain and pick over peas. Soak in 2 cups cold water for 1-4 hours. Melt butter in soup pot, saute chopped onions, carrots and celery until onion softens. Add peas and liquid to pot, add additional liquid and bring to a boil. If using ham bone or ham hock , add it now. Lower heat and simmer for 1-2 hours or until peas start to soften and

www.youtube.com/ilovetocookalot

disintegrate. Stir occasionally. Remove bay leaf and ham bone or hock if using, cut off pieces of ham and return to pot. Mash with potato masher add, ham and cook 15 more minutes to blend flavors.

PORK STEW WITH VEGGIES AND DUMPLINGS

This stew is so pretty, and very easy to make. Its healthy and showcases butternut squash. It makes a great one pot dinner, just add some bread and a salad if you desire.

- Ingredients
- 1.5 Tbs olive oil
- 20 small white mushrooms, or 8 large, quartered
- 1/2 lb pearl onions
- 2 lbs pork tenderloin, fat removed and cut into 1.5" chunks
- 1/2 cup chopped red onion
- 3 cups liquid (stock or water or a combination)
- salt and pepper
- 2 lbs peeled, seeded chopped butternut squash
- 1 Tbs cornstarch
- 1/2 cup cold water
- 1 cup flour
- 1/4 cup cold unsalted butter, cut into small pieces
- 1 tsp baking powder
- 1/2 tsp salt

- 1/2 tsp cracked peppercorns
- two minced green onions
- 1/2-3/4 cup milk
- 15-20 small broccoli florets

Directions

Heat oil in a large cast iron skillet. Saute pearl onions and mushrooms for about 5 mins., Remove and reserve. Brown pork, add chopped onion and cook 3 mins stirring, add 3 cups liquid and bring to a boil. Lower heat to a simmer and cover cook 45 mins. Dissolve cornstarch in cold water and add to stew, stir. Add squash and reserved mushrooms and onions. Bring to a boil and simmer 15 mins. In a small food processor combine flour, baking powder, salt and pepper and green onions - blend add butter in pulses to cut in. Add enough milk to make a dough. Drop by heaping teaspoonfuls around edge of stew. Place in a 400 F oven for 10-15 mins. Remove from oven and nestle broccoli florets in center. Return to oven and cook 10- 15 min or until dumplings start to turn golden brown and broccoli is tender.

SHRIMP NOODLE BOWL

This was a lot of fun. My daughter and I made dashi from scratch. What is dashi? Its a Japanese fish stock and it serves as a base for a wonderful noodle bowl, featuring shrimp and tofu...the kombu is dried kelp, and its responsible for one of the five tastes the human tongue experiences, umami (or savoriness). The other four are: bitterness, sourness, sweetness and saltiness.

Dashi:

- 8 cups cold water
- 2x4" pieces of kombu (dried kelp) wiped with a dry cloth
- 1 cup bonito flakes (dried fish flakes)
- 1" piece peeled and sliced ginger
- 1 oz mixed dried mushrooms

Udon with shrimp:

- Dashi
- 3/4 lb raw shrimp
- 1/2 cup diced firm tofu
- 2 green onions, sliced into 2" pieces and then sliced thinly lengthwise

Put kombu in a soup pot, cover with water and bring to a simmer (do NOT boil) let simmer for 20 mins, discard kombu, add bonito and ginger (off heat). Let sit for 10 mins. Drain stock, discard solids. Return stock to pot, add

www.youtube.com/ilovetocookalot

dried mushrooms and let sit for 20 mins, drain stock and reserve mushrooms, coarsely chop. Return stock to pot and heat, add shrimp and tofu cook for a few mins until shrimp turns pink, add chopped mushrooms, season with salt and white pepper. Cook Udon noodles according to package directions (in boiling water for 3 mins if using fresh udon). Place 1 cup of noodles in each serving bowl, ladle some

dashi and shrimp atop and garnish with green onions.

WHITE BEAN SOUP
Simple but delightful white bean Tuscan inspired soup.

Ingredients

- 1.5 tbs unsalted butter
- 1 tbs olive oil
- 1/2 chopped onion
- 2 stalks chopped celery
- 1/2 lb chopped baby carrots
- 2 14.5 oz cans organic white beans
- 1 qt low sodium chicken broth
- 1 bay leaf
- 1-2 fresh sage leaves, chopped
- sea salt and black pepper to taste
- 1-3 new potatoes, peeled

Directions

Heat butter and oil. add onion, celery, carrots and saute until lightly softened. Add chicken broth and beans and herbs and salt and pepper. Bring to a boil, reduce heat and simmer 30 mins. Add bay leaf and sage continue to cook about 10 mins more. Puree in blender in batches.

www.youtube.com/ilovetocookalot

If thin, add 1-2 diced new potatoes (peeled). Boil until cooked, puree until thick.

WEDDING SOUP

An Italian favorite, tiny little meatballs infuse a simple chicken broth with flavor, adding spinach and small pastas gives texture and taste to this filling and easy soup.

Ingredients

- 1 lb ground beef
- 1 egg, lightly beaten
- ½ cup italian seasoned breadcrumbs
- ¼ cup grated parmesan
- salt and freshly ground black pepper
- 6 cups chicken broth
- 1 lb baby spinach
- ½ cup arcini di pepe pasta

Directions

Combine beef, egg, breadcrumbs, parmesan, salt and pepper. Mix well with fork. Make very small meatballs (about ½" in diameter). Heat a cast iron skillet with 1 Tbs olive oil, add meatballs and brown (shake pan periodically to prevent sticking). In a large soup pot, heat broth to boiling. Add meatballs and pasta, cook 10 mins. Add spinach, lower heat and simmer five minutes more. Serve with freshly grated parmesan, if desired.

VEGGIES, SIDES, PASTA AND RICE

Side dishes usually don't take center stage by definition; they are "sides" and not the main dish, after all. However, in today's health conscious environment paying a little attention to the vegetables we serve with our meals is well worth the effort. Usually I prepare a green vegetable simply steaming or boiling, and season it with salt and pepper. Simply steamed broccoli or baby bok choy with garlic are wonderful with most meals. Sometimes, though, a more elaborate preparation is warranted – and that doesn't always translate to more work. Creamed spinach (my low fat take on it) is wonderful paired with any beef dish and eggplant parmesan makes a meal by itself. Gnocchi with spinach and cheese are my daughters' favorite dish in the whole world. Serve them with pork or beef tenderloin and a simple salad or vegetable for a memorable meal. Risotto and polenta are nice changes from potatoes – and these sides are also very versatile.

STUFFED ARTICHOKES

A simple Italian inspired stuffing jazzes up artichokes.

Ingredients

- 3 artichokes
- 1 Tbs olive oil
- 3 cloves garlic, whole
- 8 baby roma tomatoes chopped, squeeze out seeds and juice
- 1 garlic clove, chopped
- 1 tsp dried oregano
- 2 Tbs chopped fresh parsley
- 1 Tbs chopped fresh basil
- 1/2 cup breadcrumbs
- 1/2 cup freshly grated Parmesan cheese
- juice of 1 lemon
- fresh pepper
- sea salt

Directions

Boil a large pot of water, add olive oil and whole garlic cloves (peeled) add artichokes (trim top, cut off stem and snap off tough outer leaves) and cover. Cook 30 -40 mins or until tender, let drain upside down. When cool enough to handle remove choke. Combine tomatoes, herbs, breadcrumbs, cheese and lemon juice in a bowl, season with salt and pepper (can add a splash of vegetable broth if mixture is not binding together well). Stuff center of artichoke and place some stuffing between outer leaves.

www.youtube.com/ilovetocookalot

ROASTED BEETS

A simple dish -requiring very little effort . These beets taste wonderful, both the red and the gold. You can make this salad with both - but wrap them in separate foil packages to roast, and slice them separately then carefully plate up or the colors will run.

Ingredients

- 7-8 med to large beets (with greens if desired)
- 1/3 cup olive oil
- 2 tbs red wine vinegar
- 1 tsp dried tarragon
- juice of 1 orange
- 1/2 tsp salt

Directions

Cut beets off of greens, leaving about a 2 inch stem. Wrap in foil and place on a baking pan. Roast for 1 hour at 350 F. If desired, wash and chop greens coarsely and place in a covered casserole dish with 4 Tbs cold water. Place in oven with beets, for about 1 hour. Combine oil, vinegar, tarragon, orange juice and salt. Remove beets from oven and let cool slightly. Cut off stem end and tip of root end. Peel beets. Thinly slice into circles if small, or half-moons if large. Dress greens, if using, with 1/3 of vinaigrette and arrange in a ring on a large platter. Dress beets with remaining vinaigrette and pile inside ring. Serve slightly warm or chill and serve cold or at room temperature.

www.youtube.com/ilovetocookalot

BABY BOK CHOY WITH GARLIC

Another simple vegetable that pairs well with almost any main dish.

Ingredients

- 6-8 baby bok choy bunches
- 2 garlic cloves, peeled and minced
- 1 cup chicken broth

Directions

Cut core end off of baby bok choy bunches and discard. Cut leaves lengthwise and if stems are thick cut them cross wise into 1/2 " thick half-moons. Bring chicken broth to a boil in a pot large enough to hold greens, add garlic and stem ends. Boil for 3 mins, add leafy green parts and boil 3 more mins. Drain and serve.

CUBAN STYLE BLACK BEANS

A really quick take on frijoles negros - black beans with green pepper and onion. These go great with tacos, fajitas, enchiladas, quesadillas, or alone over white rice with a salad for an easy weeknight meal.

Ingredients

- 1/2 red onion, minced
- 1/2 green bell pepper, diced
- 1 Tbs olive oil
- 1 14.5 oz can black beans
- 1/2 bay leaf
- 1 tsp dried oregano
- 1/2 tsp ground cumin
- 1 tsp apple cider vinegar
- 1 tsp sea salt
- 1 tsp freshly ground black pepper
- finely chopped fresh cilantro (optional)

Directions

Heat oil in skillet and saute onions and pepper, add beans (undrained) and stir in spices, salt and pepper. Add vinegar and cook over low heat until thickened, serve garnished with cilantro and over white rice if desired.

CREAMED SPINACH

A low cal version of this steakhouse classic.

Ingredients

- 1 lb baby spinach
- 1 Tbs unsalted butter
- 1/4 chopped white onion
- 1 clove chopped garlic
- 1 tbs olive oil
- 1/8 tsp nutmeg
- salt, freshly ground black pepper
- 1/3 cup low fat sour cream

Directions

Heat oil and butter, saute onion and garlic. Add spinach, toss until cooked. Add nutmeg and stir in sour cream. Serve hot.

STEAMED BROCOLLI

A simple take on a wonderful vegetable dish.

Ingredients

- 1 head broccoli florets, florets cut into bite size pieces
- 1 cup chicken broth
- optional: 1 Tbs fresh lemon juice

Directions

Place broccoli in a steamer over a pot with chicken broth. Cover and bring to a boil, lower heat to medium and steam 5-7 mins or until broccoli is just tender. Serve drizzled with lemon juice if desired.

BRUSSELS SPROUTS

A delightfully different take on this much maligned vegetable. Even those who claim to hate Brussels sprouts love this preparation, and it is so visually striking in a pretty white serving bowl.

Ingredients

- 12 oz Brussels sprouts
- 2 Tbs melted butter
- 3 Tbs olive oil
- 1 tsp coarse sea salt
- ¼ cup chicken broth
- ¼ cup grate parmesan cheese
- Freshly ground black pepper

Directions

Wash and trim ends off sprouts. Cut in half lengthwise if small, or quarter lengthwise if large. Combine 2 Tbs olive oil with butter and salt. Toss sprouts in oil butter mixture. Heat a large nonstick skillet or well-seasoned cast iron pan over medium heat and add remaining olive oil to pan. Add Brussels sprouts, cut side down in a single layer. Cover pan loosly with foil and cook for 5 mins, remove foil and add broth and sprinkle with sea salt. Cook another 5 mins or until broth is evaporated and bottoms are well browned. Season with pepper and sprinkle with cheese, toss lightly and serve.

www.youtube.com/ilovetocookalot

CREPES WITH SPICED APPLE FILLING

An easy but very elegant dish for breakfast, or dessert – or fill with a simple cheese filling and make it a meal.

Ingredients

Crepes:

- 2 eggs
- ¾ cup milk
- ½ cup water
- 1 cup unbleached flour
- 3 Tbs melted butter
- Optional (if making a sweet filling)
- 1 Tbs sugar
- 1 tsp vanilla

Apple Filling:

- 2 granny smith apples, cored and sliced thinly
- 2 Tbs sugar
- 2 tbs butter
- 1 tsp ground cinnamon

Directions

Combine crepe ingredients in a blender and blend until smooth. Let batter sit, covered, in the refrigerator for at least 1 hour and up to 12 hours. Melt a tablespoon of butter in a medium sized cast iron skillet or non stick pan and heat

www.youtube.com/ilovetocookalot

over medium flame. Add ¼ cup batter and lift pan off flame, swirling to coat bottom with batter. After a minute or two carefully flip crepe and cook other side for about 1 minute. Remove crepe to plate. Can cook all crepes and stack once cool , wrap and refrigerate or fill immediately.

For filling: Melt butter in a small cast iron skillet, add apple slices, sprinkle with sugar and cinnamon and cook about 5 mins over medium heat or until apples soften. Place 2 Tbs of filling on bottom half off crepe and fold up in half and then over in half again. Garnish with confectioners sugar if desired.

EGGPLANT PARMIGAN

I do this all on the stovetop, so its easier and quicker., I salt the eggplant to take out any bitterness, which really makes a difference. Also, if you make extra eggplant you can snack on these while you wait for the cheese and sauce to cook once you assemble the dish. My daughter calls these "naked eggplants" the Italians call them eggplant frito.

Ingredients

- 3-4 medium eggplants, or several of the Italian smaller ones
- coarse sea salt
- 1 egg beaten with 1 Tbs water
- flour for dredging
- Italian seasoned breadcrumbs
- Tomato sauce
- Mozzarella cheese
- Parmesan cheese
- 2 Tbs olive oil

Directions

Peel eggplants and slice crosswise into ¼" thick circles. Lay these on a baking sheet lined with paper towels in a single layer and sprinkle lightly with salt, turn over and sprinkle the other side. Let sit covered with paper towel for an hour to help draw out any bitter taste. Rinse quickly in cool water and dry on fresh paper towel. Dredge eggplant in flour, egg and breadcrumbs. Fry in hot olive oil till golden on each side, turning once. Wipe skillet of most of oil, add a thin layer of sauce, top with a single layer of eggplant, more sauce and a slice of cheese on each eggplant, stack layers 2-3 more times. Sprinkle parmesan on top and cover loosely with foil. Cook over medium heat until cheese is melted and sauce is heated through.

FRITTATA

This Italian inspired egg dish is a gorgeous way to showcase a Sunday brunch.

Ingredients

- 1.5 cups thinly sliced potatoes (from about 4 medium)
- 1/2 a large onion, thinly sliced
- 4 Tbs olive oil, divided
- 5 eggs
- 1/4 cup milk
- 2 - 4 breakfast sausages, cooked and sliced
- 1 Tbs butter
- 1/2 cup grated cheese (cheddar is nice, any grateable cheese works)
- salt and pepper

Directions

Heat a cast iron skillet and add 2 Tbs olive oil. Saute onion until translucent and add potatoes. Season mixture with salt and pepper and stir to coat with oil. Cook over medium heat for 5-8 minutes, without stirring. Stir and continue to cook until potatoes soften and start to brown. Remove potatoes and onions from pan and set aside. Whisk 5 eggs together in a large bowl, add milk and cut up sausage. Add potato and onion mixture to eggs, stirring to incorporate. Wipe pan out and add 2 Tbs olive oil and 1 Tbs butter. Heat oil and butter until bubbly, swirling to coat up sides of pan. Pour egg mixture into pan, and level out top with spatula. Cook over medium flame for 5-8 minutes, until eggs start to pull away from sides of pan. Invert pan onto a large plate and slide frittata back into pan, cooked side up. Sprinkle with cheese and cook for 5 more minutes (can cover pan for last 2 minutes to melt cheese). If you are not comfortable flipping the frittata you can put it in a 350 oven for 5 mins, then sprinkle with cheese and return to oven for about 2 more minutes.

GNOCCHI VERDI

These aren't the typical potato gnocchi, they are made with ricotta and spinach and they are out of this world – sublime - amazing!

Ingredients

- 24 oz fresh baby spinach
- 2 cups whole milk Ricotta cheese
- 1 cup freshly grated Parmesan
- ~ ½ cup flour
- 1 egg
- ½ tsp salt
- ½ tsp black pepper
- ¼ cup melted butter
- Optional: 2 Tbs chopped fresh sage

Directions

Cook spinach with a small amount of water, drain and cool. Squeeze out as much liquid as possible and chop finely. Strain ricotta in cheesecloth lined strainer, weigh it down to help remove liquid. Mix spinach, ricotta, ½ cup parmesan cheese, egg, salt and pepper in a bowl. Add flour as needed to make a slightly sticky dough. Refrigerate at least 1 hour and up to 8 hours. Bring a large pot of water to a rolling boil. Add salt. Shape gnocchi into small ovals with floured hands. Place on a floured wax paper lined tray. Working in batches add gnocchi to boing water. Do not crowd. Cook until they rise to the surface. Melt butter in a heatproof serving dish (add chopped fresh sage if desired). Using a slotted spoon remove cooked gnocchi from water and place in buttered dish, in a single layer. When all gnocchi have been cooked, sprinkle dish with remaining ½ cup parmesan cheese and broil briefly to let brown in spots.

FRESH PASTA

Really, its not that hard. So very versatile and dried pasta doesn't compare. A good pasta roller is key.

Ingredients

- 2 cups semolina flour
- 2 eggs
- 1 Tbs olive oil
- ¼ cup water
- ½ tsp salt

Directions

Place flour in a standing mixer bowl and make a well in center, add beaten eggs. Using dough hook beat on lowest speed to incorporate eggs, add olive oil, salt and water. Increase speed to moderate and let mixer knead into a smooth dough. Alternatively, place flour in a mixing bowl and make a well in the center then mix in eggs, water, oil and salt by hand, and knead for 10 mins. Cover dough and let rest 20 mins. Use pasta machine to roll dough.

SOFT POLENTA WITH CHEESE

Polenta is a wonderful dish. You can serve it soft, as in this recipe, as a side in place of potatoes or rice – or you can spread it in a pan and let it firm up and cut it into squares and brush with olive oil or butter, bake briefly and top with diced tomatoes, garlic and basil as a type of crostini.

Ingredients

- 1 cup water (or milk)
- 2 cups chicken stock
- 1 cup polenta
- 1 tsp sea salt
- 2 tbs butter
- ½ cup freshly grated parmesan cheese

Directions

In a medium sauce pan bring liquids and salt to a boil. Use a wire whisk to stir in polenta, add it slowly in a thin stream. Lower heat so mixture barely simmers and continue to whisk for a few minutes. Once mixture thickens, switch to a wooden spatula and continue to stir (in one direction) for about 15-20 mins. You do not have to stir constantly, just every few minutes. Once polenta is thick enough to support the wooden spatula, add butter and cheese. Stir. Serve as is or spread into a rectangular casserole dish, using a spatula dipped in very hot water to smooth the top. Cover and let rest an hour, or refrigerate overnight. Cut into squares, brush with additional butter and broil or bake briefly. Top with topping of your choice.

www.youtube.com/ilovetocookalot

MASHED POTATOES WITH GREEN OLIVES AND CREAM CHEESE

Really easy and convenient, mashed potatoes with a twist. You can make them ahead, plus they incorporate green olives and cream cheese.

Ingredients

- yukon gold potatoes (about 3 lbs) peeled and chunked
- water to cover potatoes
- 4 oz whipped cream cheese
- 1/2 cup minced green olives stuffed with pimentos (divided)
- 2 Tbs unsalted butter
- 1/4 cup whole milk
- 1 Tbs olive water (from can or jar)

Directions

Boil potatoes in water and a little salt. Cook for about 25 mins until tender to a fork. Drain potatoes and add butter, begin to mash add milk, cream cheese, minced olives and olive water. Keep mashing until no lumps remain. Coat 8x8 glass pan with cooking spray. Layer in potatoes, make a few deep trenches with a knife and fill with remaining minced olives. Sprinkle with paprika and drizzle with butter. Place in 350 degree oven for 10 mins until golden (place under broiler for about 2 mins if needed) or cover and refrigerate up to 24 hours, bake at 350 for 30 mins or until heated through.

www.youtube.com/ilovetocookalot

POTATOES AND CAULIFLOWER WITH INDIAN SPICES

Inspired by the dish Indians call Aloo Gobi this pairing of cauliflower and potatoes is amazing.

Ingredients

- 1 small head cauliflower, broken into small florets
- 1 Tbs water
- 2 Tbs ghee
- 1 Tbs green onion, chopped (optuional)
- 1 tsp cumin seed
- 1 tsp yellow mustard seed
- 1 lb baby yukon gold potatoes, boiled in skins, cooled and peeled and diced
- 1/4 tsp ground turmeric
- 1/2 tsp ground ginger
- 1 tsp ground coriander

Directions

Heat ghee in cast iron skillet, add cumin and mustard seeds and cook over medium heat. When seeds begin to "pop" add cauliflower and a little water and cook covered for 10 minutes, until cauliflower begins to brown. Add turmeric,

www.youtube.com/ilovetocookalot

ginger and coriander, add potatoes and gently stir. Sprinkle with green onions and heat through.

POTATO GRATIN

Lovely potatoes sliced thin and layered with gruyere cheese. Do ahead factor makes it even better.

Ingredients

- 1 lb Yukon gold potatoes, scrubbed but not peeled
- 2 tsp dried thyme or 2 sprigs fresh thyme, leaves only chopped
- 2 cloves garlic, minced
- 4 oz gruyere cheese, shredded
- 1/4 cup freshly grated parmesan (optional)
- 1 cup heavy cream
- 1/4 cup chicken stock
- salt and freshly ground black pepper

Directions

Slice potato's into 1/8" thick rounds, place in a saucepan with water to cover add salt and pepper. Bring to a boil and lower to a simmer, simmer 3 mins. Drain. Butter a casserole dish (9" square or oval) layer potato's, cheese, garlic and thyme, salt and pepper, ending with cheese. Sprinkle with parmesan. Can do ahead to this point 8 hours ahead, cover and refrigerate. Bake in a 375 oven for 45 mins or until golden brown and bubbly. Let sit a few mins before serving.

ROYAL RICE

Delightful Indian inspired rice, goes great with curries and is usually adored by children and adults alike.

Ingredients

- 1.75 cups water
- 1 cup basmati rice
- 1 cinnamon stick
- 6 whole cloves
- 1/3 tsp saffron threads
- 1 tsp cardamom seeds (removed from pods)
- 3 Tbs raw cashews
- 3 Tbs currants
- 1.5 Tbs ghee
- 1 Tbs sugar

Directions

Bring water to a boil and add rice, whole cloves and cinnamon stick. Cover and lower heat. Meanwhile, dissolve saffron threads in 1 Tbs boiling water. Let sit for 10 mins. Heat ghee in a small pan and briefly saute cashews and currants until cashews are golden and currents are plump. Heat saffron water over low heat and add sugar and cardamom seeds. Stir to dissolve.
When rice is cooked, (about 20 mins.) lift lid and stir in saffron sugar water and cashews and currents. Stir and serve.

www.youtube.com/ilovetocookalot

WHITE RISOTTO

This is a great dish on its own and the basis for so many other risottos.

Ingredients

- 1/2 cup finely chopped onion
- 2 cloves finely chopped garlic
- 1 finely chopped shallot if you have one, or not
- 2 Tbs olive oil
- 1 Tbs butter
- 1 stalk celery finely chopped
- 1/2 cup white wine
- 1 cup carnaroli rice or Arborio rice
- 5 cups chicken stock
- 1/2 cup chopped flat leaf parsley
- 1/2 cup freshly grated Parmesan
- 1 Tbs additional butter

Directions

Heat olive oil and butter in a cast iron skillet. Saute onion, shallot and garlic over low heat for about 10 mins until soft but not at all browned. Stir in rice and coat each grain with oil. Add wine and stir until mostly evaporated. Add 1/2 cup hot stock and stir until almost all incorporated, continue until all stock is used and rice is creamy, still firm but not hard. Remove from heat and stir in parsley, cheese and additional butter. Serve immediately (risotto does not hold well).

www.youtube.com/ilovetocookalot

ROASTED GREEN BEANS AND CARROTS WITH BALSAMIC HONEY GLAZE

Wonderfully simple dish of roasted green beans and carrots glazed with balsamic vinegar and honey. Roasting green beans is an unusual but nice way to prepare them and a change from the standard boiling, sauteing or steaming. They do lose some of their color due to the cooking technique, but the taste is so intense and dramatic it makes up for it. With the orange of the carrots mixed in the dish, it is quite attractive albeit somewhat rustic.

Ingredients

- 1 lb green beans, washed, trimmed and snapped in half
- 1.5 cups "baby" carrots washed and cut into uniform pieces (about 1.5 inch chunks)
- 2 Tbs olive oil
- sea salt and freshly ground black pepper

For the glaze:

- 2 Tbs aged balsamic vinegar
- 1/2 - 1 clove peeled chopped garlic
- 1 Tbs honey

Directions

Preheat oven to 375 F. Line a baking pan with foil and place green beans and carrots in a single layer on foil. Toss beans with olive oil, and season with salt and pepper. Roast for 10 minutes. Mix all glaze ingredients together, remove veggies from oven and pour glaze over. Toss to coat. Return to oven and cook an additional 5-10 mins.

www.youtube.com/ilovetocookalot

SEVEN VEGETABLE STIR FRY

A really easy and fun stir-fry recipe with lots of vegetables.

Ingredients

- 1.5 Tbs canola oil
- 1/2 onion, chopped
- 1-2 cloves minced garlic
- 1 red bell pepper, diced
- 1 green bell pepper, diced
- 1/2 cup green beans, cut to 1" lengths
- 1 zucchini, sliced lengthwise in half and then into half moon slices
- 1/2 cup carrots, cut into matchsticks
- 1.5 cups broccoli florets
- 1 cup snow peas
- Salt and pepper
- 1/4 cup vegetable broth
- 1/2-1 Tbs oyster sauce
- 1/8 tsp sesame oil
- 1 Tbs toasted sesame seeds (optional)

Directions

Heat wok over med high heat, add oil and swirl to coat. Stir-fry onion for a few seconds, add garlic, bell peppers, beans, zucchini, carrots and broccoli. Stir-fry a few mins, add snow peas, vegetable broth, oyster sauce, sesame oil

www.youtube.com/ilovetocookalot

and salt and pepper. Stir-fry briefly and serve. Garnish with toasted sesame seeds if desired.

TEX MEX RICE

Easy Mexican inspired rice.

Ingredients

- 1 Tbs olive oil
- 3 cloves minced garlic
- 1/2 cup chopped white onion
- 1 cup rice
- 14.5 oz can petite diced tomatoes with mild chilis

Directions

Heat oil in pan, saute rice for 2-3 mins stirring to coat each grain. Add garlic, onion and stir to briefly cook. Add tomatoes, water and bring to a boil. Lower heat to a simmer and cook, covered for 20 mins. Serve with lime if desired.

MAIN DISHES

The main event can be easy and uncomplicated, letting the best ingredients you can afford shine through; or it can be an elaborate labor of love – but do test any new or complicated dish before you serve it to friends. Always prep for yourself, making a mise en place (chopping and dicing all your ingredients and setting them up in little bowls or piles ahead of time) and make sure to read through the recipe completely before getting started. Think about what to serve with your main dish. Sides and appetizers and dessert should complement the meal and all go together. It's not hard – rustic dishes need rustic sides, heavy food needs a light dessert, lighter fare can take a rich dessert – unless you're going for all out decadence! Whatever you choose, have fun with it!

BEEF AND BROCOLLI

This Asian inspired medley of thin sliced beef and broccoli is a favorite in our house. An easy dinner that goes together quickly, I pair this dish with a side of white or brown rice and a refreshing and even easier cucumber salad.

Ingredients

- 2 lbs NY strip steak
- 1 – 2 heads broccoli florets
- 2 cloves garlic, minced
- ½ red onion, thinly sliced into half moons
- 1" piece of fresh ginger, minced
- ¼ cup chicken broth
- ¼ cup canola oil

For marinade:

- 1 Tbs rice wine
- 2 Tbs soy sauce
- 1 Tbs water
- 2 tsp cornstarch
- 1 tsp sugar

For Sauce:

- 2 Tbs oyster sauce
- 1 Tbs soy sauce
- 2 tsp cornstarch dissolved in ¼ cup broth or water

www.youtube.com/ilovetocookalot

Directions

Place beef in freezer for 20 mins to facilitate slicing. Combine rice wine, 1 Tbs soy sauce, water and cornstarch. Slice beef very thinly across the grain (I cut away the fat). Add beef to marinade and toss to coat. Let sit at room temperature for 30 mins to an hour. Heat wok on a flame tamer, add oil. Add beef to wok in a single layer, and stir fry briefly (about 1 min) remove to plate to drain, continue until all beef is cooked. Wipe out wok and add fresh oil, if desired. Add garlic and ginger and stir fry 30 secs, add broccoli and red onion and stir fry 2 mins, add chicken broth and cover and let cook about 3 mins or until broccoli is crisp tender. Return beef strips to wok, including any juices on plate, add oyster sauce and soy sauce and cornstarch mixture, stir and cook about 2 mins more.

BI BIM BOP

Several years ago, my husband asked me to make this Korean dish. I had never even heard of it. Many attempts later he assures me I have a version that, while if not authentic, is quite close to the real thing and tastes great as well. This dish isn't complicated or hard, but it does require some time to prepare.

Ingredients

- 2 lbs NY strip steak
- 1 english cucumber
- 12 oz fresh baby spinach
- 2 cups mung bean sprouts
- eggs (1 per person eating so 2 - 4)
- 1/2 cup low sodium soy sauce
- 1/4 cup brown rice wine vinegar
- 1/4 cup sesame oil
- 3 chopped green onions
- 2 cloves chopped garlic
- 1/4 cup rice wine
- 1 tbs sesame seeds

Directions

Freeze beef for 1-2 hours to facilitate slicing. Slice beef very thinly across the grain. Marinate in: 1/4 cup rice wine, 1/4 cup soy sauce, 2 Tbs sesame oil, 1 Tbs toasted sesame seeds, crushed with a mortor and pestle or grinder, 1 clove minced garlic and 1 Tbs chopped green onion for at least 3 hours and up to 1 day. Boil a pot of water and cook sprouts

www.youtube.com/ilovetocookalot

for 30 seconds and drain and rinse in cold water. Wash baby spinach and cook till wilted, about 2 minutes. Thinly slice cucumber and sprinkle with 1 tsp salt and let sit an hour. Squeeze moisture from spinach. Mix 1/4 cup soy sauce, 1 Tbs sesame oil and 1 clove minced garlic. Divide in half and stir each half into spinach and sprouts. Mix 1 Tbs sugar, 2 Tbs rice wine vinegar and 1 tsp sesame oil. Drain cucumbers and squeeze excess moisture out. Combine sugar mixture with cucumbers. 30 minutes before serving cook a short grain to medium rice according to package directions. Heat a large wide cast iron skillet or wok with 1 Tbs sesame oil. Stir fry beef (first drain and discard marinade) 2-3 minutes until cooked rare. Set aside. Fry eggs one at a time in same skillet.

To serve, place rice in individual bowls and arrange beef, sprouts, spinach and cucumber in discrete locations on top. Place a fried egg over all if desired. Serve with Kimchi if desired.

BURRITO – CALIFORNIA STYLE

California style Burrito laden with steak, Mexican style rice, beans and cheese.

Ingredients

- 1.5 lb flank steak
- 1 Tbs olive oil
- 1/2 tsp meat tenderizer, divided
- 2 tsp southwestern dried rub OR 1 tsp each chili powder, cumin and oregano
- salt
- juice from 1/2 lime
- 1 can pinto beans, drained
- 1 can black beans, drained
- Mexican style rice, cooked
- 1 cup shredded Monterey jack cheese
- 1/2 thinly sliced red onion
- 1/2 cup red bell pepper diced finely
- 8 burrito size flour tortillas
- guacamole, sour cream, sliced green onions for garnish

Directions

Rub steak all over with olive oil, prick surface all over with a fork and sprinkle meat tenderizer on each side, rub with herbs on each side and sprinkle with lime juice. Grill on med high heat for 7 mins per side, or until medium rare. Let rest 10 mins slice thinly across the grain. Heat tortillas in a large dry skillet briefly on each side until pliable. Add filling - first rice, then beans, meat, red onion, cheese and red peppers. Roll up into a burrito. Wrap in foil. Bake in a 350 F oven for 15 mins to heat through. Garnish as desired and serve.

CAULIFLOWER CHEESE TART WITH CARMELIZED ONIONS

This rustic tart makes a wonderful vegetarian entrée for a simple dinner or a satisfying lunch. I pair it with some fresh bread and a simple salad.

Ingredients

- 1.5 Sweet white onions, sliced into paper thin half moons
- 1 Tbs butter
- 1 Tbs olive oil
- 1 medium head cauliflower, broken into small florets
- 1 Tbs olive oil
- salt and pepper to taste
- 2 eggs
- 7 oz mascarpone cheese
- 1/4 cup half n half or heavy cream
- 1/4 tsp white pepper
- 1/4 tsp nutmeg
- 4 oz gruyere cheese, grated
- 1 tsp dijon mustard
- 1/4 cup grated parmesan cheese
- 1 prepared pie crust

Directions

www.youtube.com/ilovetocookalot

Caramelize onions:
Melt butter and 1 Tbs olive oil in cast iron skillet add onions and season with salt and pepper. Cook over medium heat, stirring occasionally until golden and caramelized ~40 mins. Remove from heat and cool to room temp.

Roast Cauliflower:
Place cauliflower florets on a foil lined baking sheet and drizzle with 1 Tbs olive oil. Season with salt and pepper and toss to coat. Bake in a 400 F oven for 15 mins., stirring after 10 mins. Remove to cool and thinly slice once cool. Set aside.

Prepare crust:
Line a 9" tart pan with removable bottom with pie crust, pressing over bottom and up sides of pan. Line pan with pie weights or dried beans and bake at 350 for about 20 mins.

Prepare custard:
Beat eggs, half and half and white pepper and nutmeg in a medium bowl. Add mascarpone cheese and whisk to blend.

Assemble tart:
Spread 1 tsp dijon mustard over bottom of prepared tart crust. Layer caramelized onions on top. Layer cauliflower slices on top of onions. Pour egg custard mixture over all. Spread grated cheese on top, and sprinkle with parmesan. bake on a baking sheet in a 350 F oven for ~40 mins.

CHILI VERDE

Easy take on green chili, featuring tomatillos and pork. Skip the pork and use the sauce as a wonderful dip. With the pork this makes a fabulous filling for tacos, burritos or enchiladas.

Ingredients

- 1 lb pork tenderloin
- 4 cups chicken broth
- 4 whole peppercorns
- 1/2 bay leaf
- pinch of cumin
- 5-6 fresh tomatillos, husks removed cut in half
- 3-4 cloves garlic, unpeeled
- 1 small 12 oz can tomatillos, drained
- 1-3 jalapeños peppers, cored, seeded and diced
- 1 vidalla onion, diced
- 1 Tbs olive oil
- 1 clove fresh garlic

Directions

www.youtube.com/ilovetocookalot

In a large soup pot, combine chicken broth, peppercorns, bay leaf, cumin and tenderloin, If liquid is not enough to cover pork add additional water. Bring mixture to a boil, and lower heat to a low simmer. Cover partially and cook for about 1 hour, or until pork is tender and easily shreds. Meanwhile, lace fresh tomatillos and garlic in peel on an oiled baking sheet and broil under med high heat for 3-5 mins, until skins begin to blacken. Let cool. Place canned tomatillos, jalapeños in blender and pulse, add cooled roasted tomatillos and peeled roasted garlic. Blend. Heat olive oil in a cast iron skillet and saute onions and fresh garlic. Add tomatillo puree and cook down over medium heat for 5-10 mins. Once pork is tender, remove from liquid and let cool. When cool enough to handle using hands or two forks, shred meat into fine strips. Add meat into tomatillo mixture and heat through. Serve with buttered warm tortillas, or use as a taco or burrito filling.

PERFECT ROAST CHICKEN

How to make a moist, plump and juicy bird. This technique uses both rotation and high heat. There are countless ways to make a great roast bird, but this is my favorite.

Ingredients

- 4 ½ lb free range organic chicken
- 2 tsp fleur de sel or sea salt
- 2 Tbs softened unsalted butter
- 1 head of garlic, top 1/3 chopped off
- ½ onion, peeled
- 2 sprigs rosemary
- 2 sprigs thyme

Directions

Preheat oven to 450 F. Rinse bird and pat dry with paper towels. Use a 2" deep roasting pan which fits bird snugly. Butter pan, sprinkle salt and pepper all over chicken, including in cavity. Rub butter all over chicken. Place chicken on its side in pan and use garlic and onion to prop up. Add rosemary and thyme alongside chicken. Roast for 20 mins. Remove from oven, baste and turn to other side. Roast for 20 mins. Remove from oven, baste and turn breast side up. Roast for 20 mins. Remove from oven and baste, then lower oven temperature to 350 and roast another 30 mins (or until chicken is done, juices run clear when thigh is pierced). Take a small plate and turn upside down on a larger plate. Place bird, tail side up and breastside down on small plate, so juice will drain into the breast. Cover with foil and let rest 15 mins.

CHICKEN AL MATTONE (Flattened Chicken)

This chicken is amazing. You can use a brick wrapped in foil to weigh the bird down, but two cast iron pans and a heavy weight work well too!

Ingredients

- 1 organic, free range chicken on the small side (3.5-4 lbs)
- olive oil
- sea salt
- black pepper
- fresh thyme
- fresh rosemary

Directions

Have the butcher spatchcock the chicken (remove the backbone, flatten the breastbone so the chicken opens like a book). Season chicken on both sides with salt and pepper. Heat a large cast iron skillet until it is very hot. Drizzle with olive oil. Place chicken (open like a book) in pan – you can tuck the wings against the chicken back if this helps it fit. Place a second hot cast iron pan on top of chicken and add a 10 lb plate to this skillet if you have one, or wrap a brick in foil and use it. Let the chicken cook for about 10 mins, remove weighted pan and drizzle chicken with olive oil, flip chicken over. Add a sprig of rosemary and thyme to chicken and cover with weighted pan. Let cook another 15 mins.

CHICKEN CORDON BLEU

French inspired dish, with chicken wrapped around cheese and ham.

Ingredients

- 5 chicken cutlets, pounded thin
- 1/2 cup flour with ground pepper
- 5 oz gruyere cheese
- 5 oz Virginia ham
- 1/2 cup Italian seasoned breadcrumbs (add 1/3 cup grated parmesan cheese and pepper and salt to taste)
- egg wash (1 egg beaten with 1 Tbs cold water)
- 3 Tbs unsalted butter
- 1 tbs olive oil

Directions

Dredge one side of chicken in seasoned flour. Layer 1 oz ham and cheese on chicken (unfloured side) fold into a packet and secure with wooden toothpicks. Dredge in seasoned flour, dip in egg wash and dredge in breadcrumb mixture. Refrigerate at least 30 mins. Saute in cast iron skillet in which butter and oil has been heated. Cook until brown on both sides place in a 350 F oven for 20-30 mins.

www.youtube.com/ilovetocookalot

CHICKEN CUTLETS WITH GARLIC CHARD AND SPAGHETTI SQUASH

A complete dinner: breaded chicken cutlets with chard in garlic broth and spaghetti squash. Colorful, pleasing to the eye and wonderful to eat.

Ingredients

- 6 thin chicken breast cutlets (boneless, skinless)
- 1 cup flour
- salt and pepper
- 1 egg beaten with 1 Tbs cold water
- 1 cup seasoned breadcrumbs
- 1/2 cup grated parmesan cheese
- 1/4 cup olive oil
- 1 Tbs butter (unsalted)
- 1 medium spaghetti squash
- 2 bunches Swiss chard (red, rainbow or plain green)
- 1 cup chicken stock
- 2 cloves garlic, chopped

Directions

Dredge chicken cutlets in flour seasoned with salt and pepper. Dip in egg wash and coat with breadcrumbs mixed with parmesan cheese. Cover and refrigerate for at least 1 hour and up to 8 hours. Remove from refrigerator. Preheat oven to 350 F. Prick squash with fork all over, through rind into flesh of squash. Place squash in oven for 1 hour. Heat oil and butter in a large cast iron skillet. Wash chard and coarsely chop. Place chard, garlic and chicken broth in a

www.youtube.com/ilovetocookalot

large pot and bring to a boil. Lower heat and simmer ~15 mins. Saute chicken in hot oil/butter mixture until golden. Turn and saute on other side. Remove chicken to a paper towel lined platter when done. Remove squash from oven when soft to touch. Let cool for 5-10 mins. Handle carefully, cut lengthwise in half and scoop out seeds and discard. Scrape strands of squash into a serving bowl and season with parmesan, black pepper and Italian seasonings (oregano, basil etc). Serve with chicken breasts and drained chard.

CHICKEN PICATTA

So easy and fast this is a lovely dish served over a bed of linguine paired with a simple veggie side, like steamed broccoli or asparagus.

Dinner on the table in less than 20 minutes!

Ingredients

- 6 thin chicken breast cutlets (boneless, skinless)
- 1 cup flour
- Salt and freshly ground black pepper
- ½ cup chicken broth
- ¼ cup white wine (optional)
- Juice from 1 lemon
- 2 tbs capers, drained
- 2 tbs olive oil
- 4 tbs unsalted butter
- Fresh parsley, chopped

Directions

Dredge chicken breasts in seasoned flour. Heat olive oil and 2 Tbs butter in a cast iron skillet large enough to hold chicken without crowding. Saute chicken about 3 mins per side, remove to plate. Add broth, wine, lemon juice and 2

Tbs butter to pan and heat to boiling, stirring. Reduce by half. Return chicken to pan, add capers. Plate on a bed of pasta and sprinkle with parsley if desired.

CHICKEN STUFFED WITH FETA AND SPINACH

Easy but very pretty dish combining spinach and feta cheese, which complement one another so very well. The touch of nutmeg makes such a difference!

Ingredients

- 5 chicken cutlets
- 0.5 lb spinach
- 4 oz feta cheese, crumbled
- 1/8 tsp ground nutmeg
- Salt
- Freshly ground black pepper
- Flour, for dredging
- 1 egg beaten with 1 Tbs cold water
- 1 cup seasoned breadcrumbs mixed with 0.5 cups grated Parmesan
- 1 tsp (or 1 Tbs, if you don't mind the calories) butter
- 1 Tbs olive oil

Directions

Cook spinach in a little bit of water. Drain and squeeze out excess water. Chop spinach. Combine spinach, feta, nutmeg and salt and pepper. Pound chicken cutlets between wax paper sheets until very thin. Divide spinach mixture into 5 equal portions and place one portion in the center of each cutlet. Use chicken to encase spinach mixture and secure with toothpicks. Season flour with salt and pepper; dredge each cutlet in flour, eggwash and breadcrumbs. Cover with plastic wrap and refrigerate for at least 1/2 hour and up to 8 hours. Melt butter and oil in a heavy cast iron skillet and sauté chicken until golden on each side and cooked through. Remove toothpicks, slice chicken to show stuffing and arrange on plate.

SYRIAN CHICKEN

This chicken dish is very pretty, healthy and easy .I like to prep the veggies early in the day and then the dish goes together quite readily. Serve it over a bed of rice or egg noodles for a complete meal.

Ingredients

- 1 – 2 lbs boneless skinless chicken breasts or thighs, cut into ½" strips
- 3 Tbs chicken broth (or water)
- 1 onion chopped
- 2 cloves garlic chopped
- 2 large carrots cut into 1" matchsticks
- 1 lb thin green beans cut into 1/2 " lengths
- 1 tsp ground cumin
- 1 tsp ground coriander
- 1 tsp dried oregano
- ½ tsp dried ginger
- 4 Tbs butter, divided
- ½ cup pine nuts, optional

Directions

Melt 2 Tbs butter in a large cast iron skillet and add beans and carrots, sauté for 2 mins then add 3 Tbs chicken broth and cover. Cook over medium heat about 5 more mins or until crisp tender. Remove beans and carrots from skillet. Melt 2 Tbs butter in skillet and add onion and garlic, sauté just until onion softens. Add chicken and cook until chicken is no longer pink, stirring frequently. Sprinkle with spices and cook 2 mins more. Return green beans and carrots with their liquid to skillet and heat through, add ½ cup of pine nuts if desired. Serve over rice.

STUFFED GRAPE LEAVES

Stuffed grape leaves with rice and lamb/beef mixture. These are wonderful warm, with mashed potatoes and a veggie, or served at room temperature as part of an appetizer platter. I like them with hummus, and yogurt dip.

Ingredients

- 1 lb ground beef
- 1 lb ground lamb
- 1 cup brown or white rice
- 1 tsp salt
- 3/4 tsp ground cinnamon
- salt and freshly ground black pepper to taste
- 1 lb grape leaves
- 1 cup tomato sauce
- 1 cup water
- juice of 1 lemon

Directions

Brown meats in a hot cast iron skillet. Crumble meat, and drain fat. Cook rice in broth instead of water with salt, bring to a boil and reduce heat to a simmer, cover tightly for 40 mins. Remove rice from heat and keep covered 5 mins. Fluff with fork. Combine meats with rice (3 cups cooked rice). Add cinnamon, and salt and pepper to taste. Blanch grape leaves in boiling water, drain. Cut out tough stems from bottom of leaves. Place leaves, shiny side down on work surface. Add 1 tsp meat rice filling, shaped into a

www.youtube.com/ilovetocookalot

small cylinder, at base of leave wrap edges of leaf over and roll up into a packet. Place extra broken grape leaves in bottom of a medium sauce pan. Layer stuffed grape leaves, seam side down in a single layer. Cover with water and tomato sauce and juice of lemon. place a small plate on top to weigh down leaves. Cover pot and simmer for 45 mins. Serve grape leaves with sauce.

HAM AND NOODLE CASSEROLE

Really easy, almost instant weeknight dinner.

Ingredients

- 1/2 lb broad egg noodles
- 7 oz ham steak, cubed into 1/2" cubes
- 1/2 onion, diced
- 2 cloves garlic, minced
- 1 green onion, minced
- 1 Tbs olive oil
- 4 oz canned mushroom pieces
- 1 pkg frozen mixed vegetables
- 1 can semi-condensed cream of mushroom soup
- 1/2 cup low fat sour cream
- 1/4 cup grated parmesan cheese

Directions

Cook egg noodles in boiling water, according to package directions drain. Heat olive oil in a cast iron skillet and saute onion, garlic, green onion and ham. Combine drained noodles with sauted veggies and ham, add sour cream, soup, and season with salt and pepper. Turn into a greased casserole dish and sprinkle top with parmesan. Bake at 350 for 30 mins.

www.youtube.com/ilovetocookalot

LASAGNA AL FORNO

Classic family dish and great for a crowd. I've been making this dish forever, and many variations (spinach, instead of meat, or mushroom or just plain cheese). Everybody loves it and tries to reproduce it. Frequently, they tell me sadly that theirs just wasn't the same. Usually this is because they try to use skim milk cheese products, no boil pasta or some such thing. It's really easy, but don't stray too far. I always make at least two and freeze one.

Ingredients

Cheese Filling:

- 1 Tbs olive oil
- 1 chopped onion (vidalla or maui)
- 1 clove garlic minced
- 1 egg beaten
- 1.5 lbs whole milk ricotta cheese
- 0.5 lbs grated whole milk mozzarella
- 1/2 cup grated parmesan cheese
- salt and freshly ground pepper to taste

Meat Sauce

- 4 lbs seeded, peeled and pureed tomatoes (roma are nice)
- 2 lbs organic ground beef
- 2 tsp dried basil
- 2 tsp dried oregano

pasta:

www.youtube.com/ilovetocookalot

- 1 lb dry lasagna noodles (the kind that need pre-cooking)
- Salt

Directions

Prepare Cheese Filling:
Heat olive oil in a cast iron skillet, and saute onion until translucent. Add garlic and cook briefly. Remove from heat. Beat egg in a large bowl and add ricotta, mozzarella and parmesan. Stir well, and add oregano, parsley and salt and pepper to taste. Add onion mixture to cheese mixture. Refrigerate covered with plastic wrap until ready to use.
Prepare Meat Sauce:
Brown ground beef in a cast iron skillet, draining fat and crumbling beef. Add tomatoes and cook for about 20 minutes over low heat. Add basil, oregano and salt and pepper to taste.
Prepare pasta: according to package directions, make sure to use a large volume of boiling water, and salt same. Remove pasta while still al dente and lay on wax paper to avoid sheets sticking together.
Assemble lasagna:
In a 13x9 inch baking dish (which you first oil, or spray with cooking spray) layer some sauce, about 1/2 cup. Place 4 pieces of lasagna lengthwise sides touching in pan. Dot each pasta strip with cheese mixture, top with meat sauce. Repeat layers at least twice and up to four times. End layering with pasta, and spread sauce on top to cover (not drench). Sprinkle with parmesan cheese.

To cook: Add some thinly sliced mozzarella slices to top (about 2-3 oz) and cover with foil. Bake in a 350 oven for 20 minutes, remove foil and continue to bake about 10 mins more until cheese is melted and lasagna is bubbly. Remove from oven, replace foil and allow to sit for 10 minutes to aid in slicing.

To Freeze: cover with plastic wrap, and then foil. Freeze once dish is at room temperature. Bake frozen in a 350 for about 2 hours or until hot throughout. Don't forget to remove the plastic wrap under the foil and add some mozzarella cheese to the top first.

GRILLED HERB CRUSTED LAMB

Elegant and easy, lamb rib chops are delightful.

Ingredients

- 4 double lamb rib chops
- 1 sprig fresh rosemary
- 4 sprigs fresh thyme
- 2 cloves chopped garlic
- 1 Tbs sea salt
- 1 Tbs freshly ground black pepper
- 2 Tbs olive oil

Directions

Bring chops to room temp, coarsely chop herbs and combine with garlic, coat chops with oil, sprinkle with salt and pepper and herbs/garlic grill on high heat about 5-7 mins per side turning several times. Let sit covered in foil for 5 mins before serving.

LEEK AND CHEESE PIE

This beautiful pie is redolent with the three onion types featured -
shallots, garlic and leeks. A wonderful quiche for a hot summer night.

Ingredients

- 4-5 medium leeks, white and pale green parts only cleaned and cut in half lengthwise and then into thin half moons
- 1/2 chopped shallot
- 1 clove chopped garlic
- 2 Tbs butter
- 1 Tbs olive oil
- 1 cup heavy cream
- 3 eggs
- pinch of nutmeg
- 2 - 4 oz grated Emmentaler or Swiss cheese
- Pie crust

Directions

Melt butter and oil in a large skillet and saute garlic, shallots and leeks until softened and translucent. Beat eggs and cream in a large bowl and add nutmeg and grated cheese. Partially prebake pie crust, after pricking all over with a fork in a 350 oven for 10 mins. Add leeks to egg mixture, and pour into pie crust. Increase oven temp to 400 F and bake pie for 30 mins. Remove from oven and let cool or a wire rack to set up for 10 mins.

www.youtube.com/ilovetocookalot

MEATBALLS

Classic and loved by almost everyone, meatballs are a great choice for friends and family. I pair them with thin spaghetti, what else?

Ingredients

- 1 lb ground organic beef, 85% is fine – you want the flavor and you'll drain the fat
- 1 finely chopped clove garlic
- 1 lightly beaten egg
- ½ cup freshly grated parmesan cheese
- ½ cup Italian seasoned breadcrumbs
- 1 Tbs chopped fresh flat leaf parsley
- 1 Tbs dried oregano
- Salt and freshly ground black pepper
- Tomato sauce

Directions

Combine all ingredients and shape into walnut sized balls. Saute in a hot cast iron pan coated with olive oil until browned. Drain and place on a baking sheet in a 350 preheated oven for 20 mins. Add to sauce and heat until sauce is heated through. Serve over fresh or dried cooked pasta and pass the parmesan.

JERK CHICKEN

Don't let the long list of ingredients scare you, this is easy. The magic is in the marinade.

Ingredients

- 2 tsp ground allspice
- 1 tsp ground cinnamon
- 1/2 tsp ground nutmeg
- 1/2 tsp ground ginger
- 3 Tbs white vinegar
- 1/2 chopped red onion
- 3 chopped green onions
- juice from 1 lime
- 1 Tbs molasses
- 1/2 sprig fresh rosemary
- 1/2 stem fresh thyme
- 1 habenaro pepper, sliced (seeded for less heat, or leave them in for more fire)
- 1 Tbs olive oil
- 1/2 tsp dried habenaro pepper
- sea salt
- freshly ground black pepper
- 6 skinless chicken thighs, on the bone

Directions

www.youtube.com/ilovetocookalot

Combine all ingredients, except chicken, and process in a food processer. Pierce meat of thighs in several places, add to a ziplock bag and pour in marinade. Let marinate for several hours and grill for 20 mins per side and serve.

PORK TENDERLOIN WITH THYME SALT CRUST

Herb and garlic rubbed pork tenderloin, easy and delicious.

Ingredients

- 2 cloves coarsely chopped garlic
- 1 tsp coarse sea salt
- 1 tsp black pepper
- 1/2 tsp dried thyme
- 1 tsp olive oil
- 1 pork tenderloin

Directions

Combine garlic, thyme, salt, pepper and olive oil and rub all over pork tenderloin. Wrap in plastic and refrigerate for 4 hours (and up to 12 hours). Heat a cast iron skillet and film with olive oil. Sear pork on all sides, about 4 mins a side. Cook in preheated 350 oven for 20-30 mins or internal temp reads 170 F. Let rest under foil for 5-10 mins. Slice thinly and plate up with veggies and potatoes. Garnish with fresh parsley.

PIZZA

*Homemade pizza isn't
hard and you can choose
whatever toppings you'd
like. With only one rise it
goes together fairly
quickly as well.*

Ingredients

Pizza Dough:

- 1 cup warm water (110 F)
- 1 package active dry yeast
- 1 tsp honey
- 3 cups all purpose unbleached bread flour
- 1 tsp salt
- 1 Tbs olive oil

Toppings:

- 1 cup baby bella mushrooms, sliced
- 1/2 cup onion, sliced
- 1/2 cup green bell pepper sliced
- 1 Tbs olive oil
- 1/2 cup shredded mozzarella cheese
- 1/4 cup grated parmesan cheese
- 1/2 cup tomato sauce
- 1 tsp ground oregano
- 1 tsp olive oil or olive oil spray
- coarse corn meal to cover pizza stone

Directions

Prepare dough:
Add yeast to water
and honey. Let
proof. Combine
yeast mixture, flour,
salt, olive oil and
knead with dough
hook in standing mixer once dough forms a ball, turn out
onto floured surface and knead by hand 5 mins. Place in
oiled bowl and let rise until doubled in bulk. Punch dough
down and divide in half. Preheat oven to 400 F. Put pizza
stone in oven to heat.

Prepare toppings:
Saute mushrooms, onion and pepper in hot olive oil until
cooked
Roll out dough and place on preheated pizza stone (sprinkle
corn meal on stone first).
Prick all over with fork. Bake 5-10 mins. Spread sauce over
dough, sprinkle with cheeses and veggie toppings sprinkle
with oregano and olive oil or spray bake until cheese melts
and pie is bubbly.

VEAL SALTIMBOCA

Elegant and classic preparation. Veal cutlets pounded thin with prosciutto and sage. The name translates to "jump in the mouth" and if you do it just right, thats what happens, the dish just jumps off your plate and into your mouth!!

Ingredients

- 1 lb veal scaloppini (very thin cutlets)
- 1 cup whole milk (optional)
- 6 oz thin sliced prosciutto de parma
- 6-10 fresh sage leaves
- 1/2 cup flour for dredging
- salt and freshly ground pepper
- 2 Tbs olive oil
- 2 Tbs butter
- 2 Tbs dry white wine
- 1/4 cup chicken broth

Directions

Soak veal in milk in a casserole dish covered with plastic wrap in refrigerator for 1-2 hours, if desired. Drain veal and pat dry. Pound veal between was paper sheets, coat one side with prosciutto and sprinkle with sage. Roll loosely into a cylinder and fasten with two toothpicks. Keep cold until ready to proceed. Dredge rolls in flour seasoned with freshly ground black pepper. Melt 2 Tbs unsalted butter and 1 Tbs olive oil in a heavy cast iron skillet. Saute veal rolls on each side for 3-5 mins. until golden brown. When veal is done, remove to a platter and add Tbs white wine to skillet bring to a boil and scrape up all brown bits, pour this sauce over veal.

Note: You can also do this dish with chicken cutlets.

SALMON CAKES

Easy and so healthy. You can do these ahead and sauté just before serving.

Ingredients

- 1.5 lbs salmon fillet
- 1 lemon
- 1/2 red onion
- 1 cup carrots
- 1 egg
- 3/4 cup bread crumbs
- 2 Tbs mayonnaise (light is fine)
- 2 Tbs chopped fresh Tarragon

Directions

Poach Salmon

Coat foil with cooking spray, place salmon skin side down and drizzle with olive oil. Lay some thinly sliced lemons and 1/2 of the red onion, thinly sliced atop salmon. Encase in foil (loosely) bake on a cookie sheet at 400 F for about 8 mins or until barely done. Let cool, then remove skin and flake salmon with a fork removing any bones if needed. Chop carrots in a food processor and add 1/2 of the red onion, chop. Place mixture in a bowl, add flaked salmon, egg, bread crumbs, mayo and salt and pepper and tarragon.

www.youtube.com/ilovetocookalot

Form mixture into patties, using wet hands, refrigerate covered for at least an hour. Saute in olive oil in a cast iron skillet for a few mins per side over medium heat. Serve with tartar sauce if desired.

SHEPARDS PIE

Wonderful comfort food dish, great for a cold winter evening.

Ingredients

- 6-8 medium Yukon gold potatoes, peeled and cut in half
- 1 Tbs olive oil
- 1 onion, finely chopped
- 24 oz ground venison (or ground beef or bison)
- 1.5 cups leftover brown gravy, or high quality prepared gravy
- 1 lb frozen petite peas
- 1 lb frozen pearl onions
- 3 Tbs unsalted butter
- 1/4 cup milk
- salt and pepper to taste
- 1 Tbs paprika

Directions

Place potatoes in a pot with cold water to cover. Bring to a boil and lower heat to simmer for 20 mins or until tender. Drain potatoes and mash with butter and milk. Season with salt and
pepper. In a large cast iron skillet heat oil, saute chopped

onion and brown venison. Off heat add peas and pearl onions and gravy. Grease a casserole dish and spoon meat mixture in. Top with a layer of mashed potatoes and sprinkle with paprika. Bake at 350 for 30 mins or until heated through and lightly browned on top.

SOUTHERN FRIED CHICKEN

Real Fried Chicken. The brining and subsequent soak in buttermilk and onions lends a wonderful taste to this classic dish.

Ingredients

- 1-2 chickens, cut up
- 1 cup kosher coarse salt
- 2 cups buttermilk
- 1 onion, sliced into rings and separated
- 1 tbs black pepper
- 1 tsp Hungarian paprika
- 1 Tbs salt
- scant 1/4 tsp cayenne pepper
- 2 cups flour
- 1 cup crisco
- 1/2 stick butter

Directions

Salt chicken on both sides in a pan in a single layer and let sit (refrigerated) for 2 hours. Rinse and drain chicken. Remove skin if desired. Place chicken in a pan in a single layer and pour buttermilk over. Scatter onions on top. Cover and refrigerate for several hours. Combine flour, pepper, paprika and salt. Shake chicken to remove most of buttermilk and dredge in flour mixture. Let sit for 5 mins. to allow coating to adhere. Heat crisco and butter until hot. Fry chicken about 8 mins per side, turning once. Drain on brown paper. Serve hot or at room temperature (or my favorite, cold the next day) .

www.youtube.com/ilovetocookalot

THE PERFECT STEAK

Cooked correctly, and reliably with this technique. The perfect steak, indoors without a grill. I can't begin to imagine how many steaks I've ruined trying to cook them on the stove over the years. I finally learned how to use the cooktop and the oven in a way that allows me to reproduce wonderful steak every time!

Ingredients

- Steak – 1 inch thick cuts of high quality beef such as NY strip, porterhouse, fillet etc
- olive oil
- 1 Tbs coarse sea salt
- 1-2 Tbs freshly ground black pepper

Directions

Take the meat out of the refrigerator at least 30 minutes before cooking, (an hour is better).

Heat a large cast iron skillet (large enough to hold steaks without crowding) until it is very hot.

Season steaks with salt and pepper on both sides. Thinly coat skillet with olive oil.

Sear meat on each side for 2-3 minutes. Turn only once. Do NOT press, squish or pierce or

poke at meat. Transfer pan to a 400 F preheated oven for 7-10 minutes, depending on desired degree of doneness. Let steak rest for 5 minutes, tented in foil before serving.

www.youtube.com/ilovetocookalot

PEPPERCORN MARINATED FLANK STEAK

Easy, savory peppery marinade permeates the thin cut of beef called flank steak. Great company meal when paired with roasted rosemary potatoes and carrots, which can mostly be done ahead.

Ingredients

- Juice of 1/2 large lemon
- 2 cloves garlic, peeled
- 2 Tbs whole black peppercorns
- 1/4 cup vegetable oil (like canola)
- 1/4 cup aged balsamic vinegar
- 1 Tbs Worcestershire sauce
- 2 tbs prepared barbeque sauce
- 1.75 lb flank steak
- Olive oil for pan

Directions

Blend all marinade ingredients (everything but steak and olive oil) in a blender. pour marinade into a ziplock large plastic bag. Add meat to bag and seal, letting air out first. Rotate bag and gentle rub plastic outside to distribute marinade all over steak. Refrigerate for 3-8 hours. Remove from refrigerator 45 mins before cooking and let come to room temperature. Thinly coat a cast iron skillet with olive oil and heat over high heat. Sear steak on each side for 3-4 minutes, turning only once. Place in 400 F oven for 10 minutes, and check for desired degree of doneness. Remove from oven and tent with foil. Allow to rest 5 minutes and then slice thinly against the grain.

CHEESE AND SPINACH RAVIOLI

You can make homemade pasta for these, or buy premade fresh pasta sheet. The filling is so nice; the touch of nutmeg at the end really complements the spinach. If you make your own pasta, roll it out to the second to the last thinnest setting on your pasta machine. Too thin and the filling won't stay in the ravioli, too thick and they won't taste as heavenly.

Ingredients

- 1 egg, beaten
- 1 lb whole milk ricotta cheese, drained
- 3 oz whole milk mozzarella, grated
- 1/4 cup grated parmesan
- 5 oz cooked, drained, chopped baby spinach
- 1 tsp dried oregano
- salt and pepper to taste
- 1/4 tsp ground nutmeg
- 1 lb fresh pasta sheets

For Sage Butter

- 1 stick (1/2 cup) unsalted butter
- 2 tbs finely chopped fresh sage

Directions

Combine beaten egg, cheeses, spinach, parsley and oregano and salt and pepper and nutmeg. Refrigerate for 1 - 12

www.youtube.com/ilovetocookalot

hours. Using a ravioli mold, work with sheets of fresh pasta to encase small rounded tsp of filling. It helps if you coat the metal part of the mold with cooking spray and use cold water to brush the edges of the filled bottom pasta before placing the top sheet on. Boil in rapidly boiling salted water until pasta rises to surface and then continue cooking for ~ 3 minutes. Serve with sage butter or any simple tomato sauce. If making for a crowd, line several baking sheets with wax paper, sprinkle with corn meal and place formed raviolis on pans, in a single layer not touching until ready to boil. To make sage butter, melt butter and add sage – you can let the butter brown a bit if desired.

TUNA NOODLE CASSEROLE

Old fashioned, call it retro comfort food. Easy and lightened up a bit, with no canned anything just a basic roux.

Ingredients

- 8 oz broad egg noodles
- 4 Tbs butter
- 1/4 cup all purpose flour
- 2 1/4 cups whole milk
- 1 Tbs additional butter
- salt, pepper
- 1/2 tsp dried thyme, crushed
- 12 oz sliced baby bella mushrooms
- 1/2 cup chopped celery
- 1/2 cup chopped green onion
- 10 oz frozen baby peas and pearl onions
- 12 oz high quality canned tuna, in water
- 2 Tbs dried crispy onions (optional)
- 1/4 cup Parmesan cheese, optional

Directions

www.youtube.com/ilovetocookalot

Cook noodles, drain and rinse in cold water. Melt 4 Tbs
butter in a medium saucepan, stir in flour and cook stirring
constantly for about 2-3 mins until nutty brown .Add milk,
slowly, stirring constantly, until mixture thickens. Melt 1
Tbs butter in a cast iron skillet, add mushrooms, green
onions, celery and cook until tender, add salt and pepper.
Add vegetable mixture to sauce, stir in thyme. Drain and
brake up tuna in a large bowl. Add sauce and noodles, add
green peas and onions. Stir. Pour mixture into a greased (or
use cooking spray) 9x13 inch baking pan. Cover with
plastic wrap and refrigerate for up to 24 hours. Preheat
oven to 350. Remove plastic wrap from casserole, sprinkle
with crispy dried onions, grated Parmesan or bread crumbs.
Bake covered in foil for 20 mins. Remove foil and bake for
10 more mins.

VEGETABLE CURRY

A colorful and wonderful vegetable curry. Pair it with royal rice and naan or other flat bread.

Ingredients

- 3 - 4 medium red potatoes, boiled until barely tender, peeled and julienned
- 4 Tbs ghee
- 2 Tbs olive oil
- 2 Italian eggplants, peeled, topped and tailed and cut into 1/2 inch cubes
- 1/2 tsp turmeric
- 1/2 tsp garam masala
- 1 tsp ground cumin
- 1 tsp ground coriander
- 1/2 tsp paprika
- 1 tsp superfine sugar
- 2 Tbs water
- juice of 1 lemon
- 1 small head cauliflower, broken into bite size florets
- 8 oz cleaned baby spinach
- 6 roma tomatoes, peeled and seeded and chopped

Directions

Heat 1 Tbs ghee and 1 tbs olive oil, add potatoes and stir fry until golden brown. Remove to paper towel lined plate

www.youtube.com/ilovetocookalot

to drain. Add 1 Tbs ghee to pan, add eggplants and stir-fry over high heat until they color, remove to paper towels and drain, sprinkle with ¼ tsp turmeric and ¼ tsp garam masala. Combine remaining spices, sugar, water lemon juice in a small bowl and stir. Add 1 tbs ghee and tbs olive oil to pan, stir fry cauliflower over medium heat until it begins to brown, add spice mixture add ½ cup chicken or veggie stock and then add spinach. Cook down until spinach cooks, add tomatoes. Return eggplant and potatoes to pan. Serve over rice.

VEAL AND MUSHROOM COBBLER

Really beautiful, rustic and warm inviting dish.

Ingredients

- 3 oz sliced bacon strips
- 1 onion, chopped
- 3 cloves garlic, chopped
- 1.5 lbs veal cubes for stew
- 1 Tbs olive oil
- 3 carrots, chopped
- 2 leeks, white and pale green part, cleaned ,sliced into thin half moons
- 7 oz chopped white mushrooms
- 10 oz chopped crimini mushrooms
- 2 tsp chopped fresh thyme or rosemary or dried herbs
- Salt and ground black pepper
- 4 cups low sodium beef broth or water

For pastry leaves:

- 1 cup all-purpose flour
- 2 tsp chopped fresh thyme
- 2 tsp sugar
- 1 tsp baking powder
- 3 tbls cold, unsalted butter cut into small cubes
- 1/3 cup heavy cream
- 2 Tbs cornstarch

www.youtube.com/ilovetocookalot

- 3 Tbs cold water
- 1 egg yolk beaten with 1 Tbs milk

Directions

In a large dutch oven, brown the lardons until cooked - remove with slotted spoon and place on plate to drain. Add veal cubes and brown on all sides about 5 mins per side. Transfer to plate with bacon. Reduce heat to medium low and add oil to pot. Add onion and cook, stirring about 5 mins. Add carrots, leeks, mushrooms and garlic and cook stirring for about 5 mins. Add broth and return bacon and veal to pot. Add herbs, salt and pepper. Bring to a boil, lower heat and cook for about 45 mins, partially covered. Meanwhile, add flour, salt, sugar, baking powder and minced fresh herbs to a food processor. Cut in cubes of butter with a pulsing technique. Add heavy cream and pulse just to combine. Turn out onto lightly floured board and roll to 1/4 inch thickness. Cut into decorative shapes, place on a plate and cover refrigerate until ready to use.

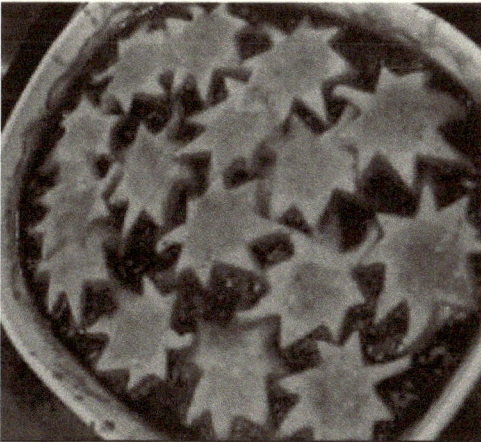

Heat oven to 350. Combine 3 Tbs water and cornstarch, heat stew to boiling and stir in cornstarch mixture boil 1 min. Ladle the veal stew into

www.youtube.com/ilovetocookalot

a large casserole dish and arrange the pastry cut outs atop, overlapping but allowing some space for stew to vent steam. Brush pastry with egg wash. Bake (on a baking sheet to catch spills) for 30 -35 mins. Cool for 10 mins on a wire rack.

VEAL CANNELONI

Delicate homemade pasta encases a rich filling of veal, sausage and herbs.

Ingredients

- Homemade Pasta

Filling

- 1 small onion, finely chopped
- 1 small shallot, finely chopped
- 1 garlic clove, finely chopped
- 2 Tbs unsalted butter
- 1 lb ground veal
- 1 hot sausage, casing removed
- ½ cup chopped fresh parsley
- 1 beaten egg
- ½ cup grated mozzarella
- ¼ cup grated parmesan
- 2 Tbs tomato paste
- 1 tsp dried oregano
- 1 tsp dried basil
- salt and freshly ground black pepper

Directions

Use pasta machine to roll dough to 2nd to thinnest setting. Cut sheets into 5" squares. Cook 2 mins in boiling water and lay flat on wax paper to cool briefly.

www.youtube.com/ilovetocookalot

Saute onion, shallot and garlic in melted butter over medium heat. Add veal and break up with wooden spoon. Add sausage, and break up meat. Cook until meat is cooked through. Remove from heat. Stir in remaining ingredients and let cool to room temperature. Prepare a casserole dish (rectangle is best) by spraying with cooking spray or lightly coating with olive oil. Place a thin layer of tomato sauce on the bottom. Using about 2 Tbs of filling per pasta square, make cannelloni. Place filling in lower third of pasta square and roll up, encasing filling. Place seam side down in pan, touching in a single layer. Pour a thin layer of tomato sauce on top and sprinkle with parmesan cheese. Bake at 350 for 20-30 mins or until bubbly and heated

through.

SHOW STOPPER MAINS

Every once in a while when you gather with special friends and family you want to do something beyond amazing – something that really wows people. Usually I subscribe to the notion that simple is best, letting good ingredients shine without a lot of fancy preparation but sometimes I like to really go to town. So here are just a few ideas for some truly memorable meals, including some of the recipes I use for holidays

CRISPY FRAGRANT DUCK

You need to start this 2 days ahead, and this is one of those recipes you really should read all the way through before doing (like they say about all recipes but usually we don't)! Very special dish similar to Peking duck. All the fat is rendered out leaving a very crispy skin and meat so tender it falls off the bone.

Ingredients

- 1 4.5-5.5 lb duck
- 6 Tbs Sichuan Peppercorn salt
- 1 Tbs Five Spice Powder
- 2 Tbs Chinese Rice wine
- 6 1/8" thick slices of fresh ginger
- 4 scallions cut into 2" lengths
- 12 cups canola oil
- 2 Tbs dark soy sauce
- 1/3 cup flour

Directions

You need a wok, a pie plate, a rack, a good quality baster and an electric fan

Prepare duck:

Cut of wing tips, remove excess fat, rinse in cold water and pat duck dry. Press down on breastbone to break it and flatten duck. Heat peppercorn salt and five spice powder in

www.youtube.com/ilovetocookalot

a dry skillet just until fragrant. Remove from heat and let cool. Measure 3 Tbs and rub all over duck inside and out. Let duck marinate in this rub chilled for 8-24 hours.

Steam duck:

Drain duck and place in a glass pie plate. Rub rice wine over duck, place 1/3 of the ginger and scallions in duck cavity and sprinkle the rest on top. Fill wok with 1-2 inches of water set a rack in wok and place duck on pie plate on top of rack. The rack should not touch the water, adjust as needed. Remove duck and pie plate. Bring water to a boil and CAREFULLY place duck in pie plate on rack and cover wok. Reduce heat to moderate and steam duck 2 hours, checking to siphon off fat with baster and adding more boiling water as needed. Initially the duck will give up a lot of fat, so you need to use the baster to take it away frequently. Remove duck, discard ginger and scallions drain duck and let cool 15 minutes.

Dry Duck:

Place duck in front of an electric fan and air dry duck for 4 hours

Fry Duck:

Brush duck with soy sauce and sprinkle with flour. Heat oil in wok to 375 , fry duck (CAREFULLY) for 2 minutes,

www.youtube.com/ilovetocookalot

turn over and fry 1 minute. Remove duck to drain on brown paper. Heat same oil to 400 F and fry duck again, 30 seconds per side.

OK - your done. You eat this with hoisin sauce with sesame oil and sugar added to taste, and chinese pancakes to wrap the duck pieces in, you can also garnish with green onion brushes.

You don't carve this duck, it just shatters into pieces, you can use chop sticks or a fork. Also, after steaming the duck it does not look very attractive - don't worry after the frying it looks gorgeous!

PIEROGI

I think of these as Polish raviolis, but that's not really fair because they are wonderful in their own right! We have these on Christmas eve with Kielbasa sausage and plenty of butter sautéed onions.

Ingredients

Dough:

- 4 cups all purpose unbleached flour
- 2 egg yolks
- 2 Tbs unsalted butter, softened
- 2 Tbs sour cream
- pinch of salt
- 1.5 cups potato water

Fillings:

For Potato, onion and cheese:

- 7 large red skinned potatos
- 2 large onions
- 1/4 lb butter
- 1/2 pound grated colby cheese

For cottage cheese filling:

- 1 cup dry cottage cheese (add to half of potato filling)

www.youtube.com/ilovetocookalot

Directions

Peel and cook potato's in cold water to cover, bring to a boil and lower heat simmer until cooked about 20 mins. Drain potaoes and RESERVE cooking water. Saute diced onions in melted butter until soft. Combine onions with potato's and colby cheese. Mash together and season with salt and pepper. If cottage cheese filling is desired, add cottage cheese to ½ of potato filling. Measure flour into a large bowl and make a well in the center. Combine softened butter with sour cream and egg yolks. Add to flour and incorporate. Add 1.5 cups reserved potato water and cut in to make a soft dough. Knead dough until firm, form into a ball and cover with a kitchen towel and let rest 10 minutes.

Roll out dough on a floured board and cut into circles and fill, pinching edges with floured fingers to seal. (I use a scant tsp of filling per circle). Filled pierogis look like half-moons. Drop

into a large pot of boiling water, 6 at a time. When they rise to the surface cook for 2 more minutes. Remove with a slotted spoon and place on wax paper lined cookie sheets in a single layer, not touching one another. You can freeze them at this point, and when frozen remove from wax paper and place in a ziplock bag for up to a month. Or, you can refrigerate them for a few hours, or cook right away. Melt 2 Tbs butter in a cast iron skillet and sauté another sliced

www.youtube.com/ilovetocookalot

onion in butter, add pierogis and saute on each side until golden. If freezing, thaw slightly before sautéing.

Note: Do not make pierogies with a dough cutter any bigger than 3.5" in diameter, or you will be making "peasant" pieorigi!!

BEEF WELLINGTONS

I usually make these during the holidays - but they are great entertainment food any time of year. The dish is very labor intensive BUT you can break up the individual parts over several days and the whole thing can be prepared ahead of time so that on the day of your dinner party all that remains is hands off baking for about 50 mins. You need to start these at least 2 days before you plan to serve them, but you can do them a whole week ahead if you desire. They are truly spectacular and also quite decadent and delicious.

Ingredients

- 3 pkgs puff pastry (1 lb each)
- Flour for rolling

Mushrooms:

- 2 large portabella stems removed
- 6 Tbs olive oil
- 2 cloves fresh garlic, minced
- 1 tsp fresh thyme, chopped
- 1 tsp fresh rosemary, chopped

Onions:

- 4 Tbs butter
- 3 medium Vidalia onions, thinly sliced
- 0.5 cup dry sherry or white wine
- Salt and pepper

Spinach:

- 12 cups baby spinach (14 oz)
- 2 Tbs butter

Beef:

- 6 portions beef tenderloin 5-6 oz each
- 6 oz Maytag blue cheese
- Salt and pepper
- ~1/4 cup olive oil

For assembly:

- 2 eggs whisked with 1 tsp cold water
- 2 eggs whisked with 1 tsp cold water

Directions

1)Roll and cut pastry: thaw puff pastry and roll each sheet 3/16 inch and cut a 10 inch round out of each sheet. Cut small decorative shapes from scraps. Layer the pastry rounds between wax paper wrap tightly in plastic wrap and freeze.
2) Cook mushrooms: toss mushrooms in oil, garlic and herbs. Cover and marinate in refrigerator for 2 hours. Remove from oil and season with salt and pepper. Heat a heavy skillet and add a thin film of olive oil. Sear mushrooms 5 minutes per side. Let cool and cut into 1/2 inch wide long strips. Chill.
3) Onions: Melt butter in a heavy pan. Add onions, lower heat and cook slowly stirring occasionally about 30-40 mins. Add the sherry and cook until dry. Place in a strainer

over a bowl, cover and chill.

4) Spinach: melt 2 Tbs butter in a large saute pan and cook spinach about 5 mins. Tossing to cook evenly. Place in an ice bath to shock the color. Drain and squeeze out as much water as possible. Wrap in plastic and chill.

5) Divide cheese into 6 equal portions.

6) Sear fillets: season with salt and pepper put 1/8th inch of olive oil in a cast iron skillet and heat over very high heat. Sear meat 2 mins per side (you are not cooking through at this point) Chill at least 2 hours and up to 24.

7) To assemble: for each one: work quickly. Remove a pastry round from freezer and cut out edges to form a cross with a 4x3 rectangle in the center.

8) Take 1/12th of the spinach and place in center. Top with 1 oz blue cheese, 1/6th of the onions, 1 beef portion, 1/6th of mushrooms in a flat layer and 1/12th spinach. Flatten layer as you go.

9) Brush egg wash over all exposed pastry and fold up package, sealing completely. Egg wash package and place seam side down on wax paper. Decorate with pastry scraps if desired and egg wash again. Place in uncovered in freezer for 1 hour, remove from freezer, wrap completely in plastic wrap and return to freezer at least 12 hours.

10) To cook: DO NOT THAW. Preheat oven to 400. Egg wash Wellingtons and place on a lightly greased baking sheet. Cook for 20 mins. Reduce oven temp. to 350 and continue to cook about 30 more minutes or until internal temp of meat is 110 F. Remove and let rest 5-10 mins. Cut in half to display layers and serve.

TIMPANO

This is one impressive Italian dish – and really not that hard to make if you do it in stages! Pastry encases layers of pasta, meatballs, chicken, cheese and peas all covered in tomato sauce. Pastry, meatballs, chicken and sausage can all be made ahead .

Ingredients

For Pastry

- 2 cups all purpose unbleached flour
- 1 tsp salt
- 2 sticks (1 cup butter) cut up and placed in freezer for 15 mins
- 2 eggs

For Meatballs

- 1 lb ground beef
- ½ cup italien seasoned breadcrumbs
- ¼ cup grated parmesan cheese
- 1 tsp dried oregano
- 1 egg
- Salt and pepper

For Chicken

- 2 chicken breasts, boneless and skinless
- 2 Tbs olive oil
- ½ chopped onion
- ¼ cup white wine
- 1 Tbs chopped garlic

- Juice of 1 lemon

Other

- 1 lb mezze penne or other tubular pasta
- ¼ cup chopped fresh flat leaf parsley
- 1 cup grated mozzarella cheese
- 2 cups tomato sauce
- 3 Italian sausage
- 1 cup frozen green peas

Directions

Prepare Pastry – combine flour and salt in a food processor and cut in chucks of cold butter, pulsing, add butter in small amounts. Once butter is cut in add eggs and continue to pulse until dough forms (add cold water 1 Tbs at a time if necessary to form dough). Form into a ball and refrigerate at least 1 hour and up to overnight. Divide dough into two pieces one slightly larger than the other. Roll larger "half" into a 14" circle and line a buttered 10" spring form pan with dough, covering bottom and sides of pan. Cover with plastic wrap and refrigerate. Roll remaining dough into an 11" circle and placed on lightly floured parchment lined pan or plate and cover and refrigerate. Prepare meatballs – combine beef and all other ingredients, shape into walnut size balls and sauté in cast iron skillet in 1 Tbs olive oil. Prepare chicken – melt butter in olive oil and sauté onion and garlic, add chicken and cook till golden on each side and cooked through. Pour in white wine and lemon juice, raise flame and cook till wine

evaporates. Prepare sausage – cook in cast iron skillet, puncturing with fork in spots to prevent bursting , turn occasionally. Drain on plate and when cool cut into 2 inch chunks.

When ready to prepare Timpano bring meatballs and chicken to room temperature. Cook pasta according to package directions, drain and dress with about ¼ cup of tomato sauce. Remove pastry lined pan from fridge and place on a large baking sheet. Preheat oven to 350 F. Layer pasta in bottom of pastry shell, just about a single layer, cut chicken breasts into ½" thick thin strips and layer ½ of chicken on pasta, layer ½ of meatballs and ½ of sausage, add ½ cup frozen peas, ½ cup cheese and 1 Tbs parsley. Cover with ½ cup sauce and press layer down to flatten and pack it. Repeat layer and end with the start of a third layer – just pasta and sauce. Remove top crust from fridge and place over timpani, cutting edges to fit. Crimp inside the pan to seal edges and facilitate removal. Cut four vents in top with a sharp knife and bake for about 45 mins or untol heated through. Remove from oven and let sit for 10 mins to set. Remove outer edge of pan, place on a pretty serving dish and cut like a pie. Serve with additional sauce if desired.

THANKSGIVING

*This wonderful holiday mandates the same menu in our
house, something I simultaneously enjoy and regret –
always wishing I could get more creative yet also loving the
predictability of this delicious meal. I plan ahead, and aim
to have much of the work done before the actual day. The
bulk of the menu stays constant – chestnut stuffing, roasted
turkey, turkey gravy, cranberry sauce, candied sweet
potatoes and pumpkin pie – but I do vary the appetizers
and vegetable side dishes. Usually I make mashed potatoes
as well and a green bean dish garnished with sliced
almonds sautéed in a little butter. Sometimes I do Brussels
sprouts with diced bacon or I will make both green veggies
if the crowd warrants. Also, I usually add a platter of
Thanksgiving themed cookies with the pie, and sometimes
do a pecan or mincemeat pie.*

*A few days before the big meal, I shop for all non-
perishables. I plan on how to set the table – what serving
dishes to use, etc. Two days before I make the cranberry
sauce and the sweet potatoes. The day before I make the
stuffing – and I usually make two, one with sausage and
one without. I make the cookies and pie the day before as
well. All this advance preparation makes the actual day a
great time to visit with family and friends, basically just
attending to the turkey and gravy – I let others help with
the mashed potatoes and vegetables, and work on
presenting everything as attractively as possible. For*

www.youtube.com/ilovetocookalot

appetizers I do whatever I am in the mood for – roasted and spiced nuts are almost always part of my holiday hors d'oevres and then either a veggie platter with dip, some cheese and grapes or crackers.

PUMPKIN PIE

Sure you can buy a sugar pumpkin but canned pumpkin is a wonderful product. Make this pie a day or two ahead. Also keep in mind this makes a wonderful addition to breakfast the day after the holiday!

Ingredients

- ¾ cup sugar
- ½ tsp ground ginger
- 1 tsp ground cinnamon
- ¼ tsp ground nutmeg
- ½ tsp ground cloves
- ½ tsp salt
- 2 eggs, beaten
- 12 oz evaporated milk
- Pure pumpkin puree

Directions

Combine sugar and spices and salt in a small bowl. Add pumpkin to beaten eggs in a medium bowl, and stir to combine. Add sugar spice mixture and stir thoroughly. Add evaporated milk, in small amounts, stirring to combine. I usually use a little less than the 12 oz, maybe about 10. Pour mixture into a pie shell, place on a baking sheet. Bake in 350 F preheated oven, for about 50 mins. Check after 20 mins to see if edges are browning, if so cover pie edge with tin foil. Use a clean knife to test if pie is done (insert into center of pie and if it comes out clean pie is done).

www.youtube.com/ilovetocookalot

SPICED CRANBERRY SAUCE

Super simple, and so lovely. Super fine sugar isn't necessary but it dissolves so beautifully. Keep in mind that this thickens as it cools. Make ahead and keep ready to serve in the refrigerator – but please take it out 30 mins ahead of time so the flavor can truly be appreciated.

Ingredients

- 1 cup super fine sugar
- 1 cup water
- ½ cinnamon stick
- ¼ tsp ground cloves
- Peel from 1 orange or 1 lemon, 2 Tbs juice from corresponding fruit
- Fresh cranberries (12 oz)

Directions

In a small pot combine water, sugar and spices. Bring to a boil, stirring to dissolve sugar. Add cranberries to pot and lower heat. Cook for 10 mins, stirring occasionally. Pour into a pretty bowl (remove cinnamon stick) and let cool. Can keep in refrigerator for 3 days.

CANDIED SWEET POTATOES

Can make these a day or two before hand and heat in the oven while the turkey rests. No marshmallows here, just delicious sweet potatoes.

Ingredients

- 4 sweet potatoes
- 1/3 cup packed Brown sugar
- 2 Tbs maple syrup
- Nutmeg
- ½ cup Butter
- 1 tsp Vanilla

Directions

Boil potatoes for about 20 mins or until fork tender. Remove from water and peel. Cut into large chunks. Melt butter with brown sugar, maple syrup and vanilla. Butter a pretty casserole dish. Toss sweet potatoes in butter syrup mixture; grate some fresh nutmeg in, if available. Place in casserole dish. Bake at 350 for 30 mins. These can be made ahead and refrigerated covered for up to 1 day, if baking cold add 15 mins to cooking time.

CHESTNUT SAUSAGE APPLE STUFFING

This dish can be made the day before, and kept covered in the fridge. Heat it up while the bird rests! The sausage is optional and if you use vegetable broth instead of chicken broth you will have a delectable vegetarian treat.

Ingredients

- ½ cup butter
- ½ lb pork sausage with sage
- 2 cups chopped celery
- 2 cups chopped vidalla onion
- 2 peeled granny smith apples, cored and diced
- Roasted chestnuts (roast them your self or buy peeled in a jar) diced (2 cups)
- 2 cups chicken broth
- 14 oz bag dried stuffing (or 1 lb bread, cubed and toasted)
- 2 sprigs fresh thyme
- 4 leaves fresh sage

Directions

Melt butter, sauté onion and celery until softened. Brown sausage in a separate skillet, drain fat and add apple to sausage – sauté briefly. Add to celery and onion mixture. Add chicken broth and bring to a boil. Take off heat, add cubed bread, stir in chopped sage and chopped thyme. Toss together and cover and let sit. Butter a large casserole dish and place stuffing in dish. Cover with foil and refrigerate overnight. Heat in a 350 F oven, covered, for about 30 minute then remove foil and cook another 30 mins. or until heated through.

GLORIOUS ROAST TURKEY

Using a cheesecloth dipped in melted butter and savory herbs lets the bird stir wonderfully moist, it also imparts a beautiful deep mahogany color to the skin. Take care not to let the cheesecloth dry out and do not overcook your bird!

Ingredients

- 1 14-16 lb organic turkey
- 1 stick (1/2 cup) unsalted butter
- ¼ cup fresh sage leaves
- 2 tsp sea salt
- Poultry seasoning
- Freshly ground black pepper
- Chicken broth

Equipment

- Roasting pan to hold turkey
- Rack for roasting pan
- Large piece of cheesecloth

Directions

Preheat oven to 400 F. Melt butter and add salt, pepper and sage leaves. Add 1 Tbs poultry seasoning if desired. Soak cheesecloth in butter herb mixture, place washed and dried turkey on rack in roasting pan. Salt outside of bird and inside cavity. Add a quartered peeled onion to cavity if desired. Place moistened cheesecloth on top of turkey

www.youtube.com/ilovetocookalot

pressing to fit it snugly all over bird. Place turkey in oven, baste every 30 mins. Lower oven to 350 after first 30 mins. Cook for about 3 hours or until a thermometer reads at least 165 F inserted into thigh and then breast. Be careful to keep the cheesecloth moist on the bird, use chicken broth if not enough juice is available to baste in the early stages of cooking, after 2 ½ hours carefully peel cheesecloth off of turkey and discard. Once turkey is done, let sit tented with aluminum foil for at least ½ hour. This resting period is essential; it lets the juices stay in the meat making for a moist and succulent bird.

DESSERT

So often a simple bowl of ripe fruit ends a meal quite beautifully – but sometimes we want a little bit more. What follows are the various desserts I draw on for special occasions, for company or just for fun with my family. I always try to use the best ingredients I can find, pure vanilla extract, a whole vanilla bean when warranted, the highest quality chocolate I can afford. I prefer superfine sugar to standard granulated, but if you can't find it or don't want to spend the little bit extra it costs, just take your standard granulated white sugar and blitz it in a food processer for a few seconds. It mixes into things like egg whites and sifts into flour more readily and it dissolves faster in liquids.

The type of meal I am serving usually guides my choice of dessert. In general I aim for balance, so a very heavy robust meal gets a lighter dessert but sometimes total decadence is called for!

Cookie platters are fun to prepare, and I like to include several types – usually at least one type of biscotti and a softer cookie. Biscotti has the added advantage of keeping very well – so you can always have some on hand.

For an elegant ending to any meal panna cotta is one of my favorite deserts. You can make it ahead of time and if you unmold it on pretty dessert plates and dress it up with a simple berry coulis it is amazing to behold as well as eat.

Pies are always welcome – and a store bought high quality crust makes them easy to prepare. Whatever you choose, a homemade dessert adds a festive touch to dinner, that won't be forgotten!

ALMOND BISCOTTI

A classic biscotti, this recipe uses no butter or oil in the dough to make for a low fat, low cal and delicious cookie, which is wonderful dipped in coffee. These keep very well in an air-tight container for 2 weeks or more and are great to ship to family and friends.

Ingredients

- 1 cup raw almonds
- 2-3 eggs (i ended up using 3) beaten with extracts (1 tsp vanilla extract and 1/2 tsp almond extract)
- 2 cups all purpose flour
- pinch of salt
- 1 cup white sugar
- 1 tsp baking powder

Directions

Preheat oven to 350 F. Roast almonds in a single layer on a baking sheet for about 10 mins or until toasted. Let cool then coarsely chop. Lower oven temp to 300 F. Combine flour, salt, sugar and baking powder and beat with electric mixer at low speed (or sift dry ingredients together in a large bowl). Slowly add eggs until a soft and crumbly dough forms fold in almonds Divide dough in half and shape each half into a 10 inch by 2 inch log. Place on parchment lined baking sheet, or buttered sheet, 3 inches apart as log will spread while cooking. Bake for 30-50 mins or until firm to the touch. Remove to wire racks to cool for 10 mins. Using a serrated knife cut into 1/2" slices on the diagonal. Raise oven to 350, Return cookies to baking pan and either stand up on edge, and bake for 10 mins or until toasted, or place on one side and bake for 10 mins, then turn and bake 10 mins more on other side.

AMBROSIA

Food of the Gods! So easy and simple, but the combination of fresh orange and dried coconut is beyond outstanding. This is the perfect instant desert! [Note: raw honey is not recommended for infants]

Ingredients

- 1 navel orange, peeled, and white pith removed diced into 1/2 inch dice
- juice from remaining orange pieces
- 1/4 cup organic finely shredded coconut
- 1 Tbs honey (clover honey)
- 2 sprigs fresh mint leaves

Directions

Combine orange cubes, juice, coconut and honey. Stir gently, garnish with fresh mint, increase servings as desired.

ANGEL FOOD CAKE

A Classic - angel food cake, so pretty and so easy and light.

Ingredients

- 12 egg whites
- 1.5 tsp cream of tarter
- 0.5 tsp salt
- 1 tsp vanilla extract
- 1 tsp almond extract
- 1 cup cake flour
- 1.5 cups sugar, divided

Directions

Beat egg whites until frothy, add cream of tartar and extracts Beat egg whites until stiff peaks form (do not let get dry) add 3/4 cup sugar slowly (2 Tbs at a time) beating after each addition. Sift together flour, salt and ¾ cup sugar. Sift a second time. Remove bowl from beater and sprinkle 1/4 of flour/sugar/salt mixture over top of egg white batter fold in, add remaining flour mixture 1/4 at a time folding in. Spoon into 10 inch angel food tube pan and level surface cook for 35 mins invert over a bottle until cool. Remove to serving platter serve with strawberries or plain.

APRICOT ALMOND TART

A beautiful simple tart, this dish combines fresh apricots with almonds.

Ingredients

tart crust

- 1 cup flour
- 1/3 cup toasted and cooled almonds
- 1/4 cup sugar
- 1/2 tsp salt
- 1/2 cup chilled butter cut into small 1/2" cubes
- 1 egg yolk
- 1 tsp almond extract

tart filling

- 1/2 cup apricot preserves
- 3/4 cup sugar
- 1/3 cup toasted and cooled almonds
- 1/2 tsp cinnamon
- 10 – 12 large apricots, halved and pitted

Directions

For crust:
Blend flour, almonds, sugar and salt in a food processor until nuts are finely chopped. Add butter and cut in using on/off pulsing. Add 2 Tbs cold water, egg yolk and extract. Blend together. Gather dough into a ball and press into

bottom and up sides of a 9" tart pan with removable bottom. Chill 30 mins. Set rack at lowest position in oven. Preheat to 375. Stir preserves over low heat to melt, strain through a fine strainer. Finely grind almonds and 1/2 cup sugar and cinnamon. Spoon mixture over bottom of crust. Arrange apricots, rounded side up, snugly in crust. Brush with 1/2 of melted preserves and sprinkle with remaining sugar. Bake about 1 hour or until fruit is tender. Cool 1 hour on wire rack. Warm remaining preserves and brush over tart if desired.

APPLE CRISP

This works with blueberries as well, just toss 3 cups of blueberries with 2 Tbs flour and 1 Tbs lemon juice.

Ingredients

- 1 cup sifted all purpose unbleached flour
- 1/2 cup sugar
- 1 tsp baking powder
- 1/4 tsp salt
- 1 tsp ground cinnamon
- 1 egg
- 5 granny smith apples, peeled cored and cut into 1.5" chunks
- 1 golden delicious apple, peeled cored and cut into 1.5" chunks
- 1/4 - 1/2 cup melted unsalted butter
- 1/2 tsp cinnamon

Directions

Butter a casserole dish, preheat oven to 350 F, place apples in casserole dish. Combine flour, sugar, baking powder and salt and cinnamon - add egg and stir. Sprinkle topping over apples and drizzle surface with melted butter.

www.youtube.com/ilovetocookalot

Sprinkle with additional cinnamon if desired. Cook for 40 - 50 mins, or until golden brown on top. Serve warm, alone or with vanilla ice cream, yogurt or sour cream.

BISCOTTI DI REGINA

Italian Sesame seed cookies, these are amazing when made with the pure white fat from roasting a goose.

Ingredients

- 1.5 cups all purpose flour
- 2/3 cup granulated sugar
- 1 tsp baking powder
- 6 Tbs goose fat (white part only)
- 1 egg, beaten
- 1/2 tsp vanilla
- 1/2 tsp salt
- 1/2 cup milk
- 1/2 cup sesame seeds

Directions

Combine all ingredients except milk and sesame seeds. Stir to make a soft dough. Preheat oven to 375. Shape dough into small logs (about 1.5 inches long) and dip in milk then roll in seeds.
Bake for ~ 10-15 mins. Cool on a wire rack.

BLUEBERRY PIE WITH STARS

Great fun for 4ᵗʰ of July but you could use any shapes, or just do a top crust.

Ingredients

- Pie crust
- 4 cups blueberries
- 1/4 cup instant (minute) tapioca
- 1 Tbs lemon juice
- 1 cup sugar
- 1/4 tsp ground cinnamon
- 2 Tbs unsalted butter
- 1/4 cup very cold butter cut in small pieces
- 1/2 cup flour
- 2 Tbs sugar
- 1-2 Tbs ice cold water

Directions

Preheat over to 400 F. Mix berries with tapioca, sugar, lemon juice and cinnamon. Let sit 15 mins. Pour into crust and dot top with butter. Bake in 400 over for about 1 hour, use foil to cover edges if they start to brown too much. Let pie cool completely on wire rack.

Combine flour, sugar and a touch of salt in food processor. Cut in butter. Add water and process until dough forms a ball. Shape into a flattened circle and refrigerate 1 hour. Roll out on lightly floured surface and cut out stars in two

www.youtube.com/ilovetocookalot

sizes, 2 inches and 1 inch. Bake on ungreased cookie sheet at 350 for about 1o mins or until edges start to turn golden. Cool on wire rack. Randomly arrange stars on top of cooled pie.

BUTTERSCOTCH PUDDING

A classic homemade pudding, with very intense butterscotch flavor.

Ingredients

- 1.5 cups packed dark brown sugar
- 2 Tbs unsalted butter
- 3 Tbs cornstarch
- 4 cups milk, divided (whole or 2%)
- 1/4 tsp salt
- 4 eggs beaten

Directions

Melt butter and sugar over low heat in a medium pan. Turn heat to high and cook until bubbly. Add 3 cups milk, stirring to melt any hardened sugar. Cook for 5 mins. Combine cornstarch and remaining 1 cup milk to make a paste and stir in. Cook until mixture starts to thicken, about 6-8 mins. Add salt. Add a little bit of hot mixture to eggs, stirring and a little more, stirring to warm eggs. Add eggs to hot mixture and whisk constantly. Bring to a boil and continue to cook about 5 mins more until mixture thickens. Pour into individual ramekins and refrigerate until chilled. Serve with whipped cream if desired.

MINI CARROT CUPCAKES

A fast and easy take on carrot cake, scaled down to a tiny treat!

Ingredients

- 2 eggs, room temperature
- 1 cup sugar
- 1/2 cup vegetable oil
- 1/4 cup buttermilk
- 1/2 tsp vanilla extract
- 2 cups grated peeled caroots (about 1.5 lbs)
- 1/2 cup raisins
- 1.5 cups all purpose flour
- 1 tsp baking powder
- 1/2 tsp baking soda
- 1 tsp cinnamon
- 1/4 tsp salt

Directions

Combine eggs, sugar, oil, buttermilk and vanilla extract and beat with a paddle attachment on a mixer or by hand until well combined. Sift together flour, baking powder, soda, cinnamon and salt. Add 3/4 of flour mixture, in batches, to oil mixture stirring to combine.

www.youtube.com/ilovetocookalot

Add carrots and raisins to remaining flour and toss to coat. Fold in carrots and raisins, into batter. Combine well. Line mini muffin pans with mini baking liners and add 2 tsp to each muffin paper. Bake for 10-12 mins at 350 F. Cool completely before frosting (optional).

CHEESECAKE – NEW YORK STYLE

A classic and always big on the wow factor. Start this a day ahead of time so it has time to chill.

Ingredients

for crust:

- 2 cups graham cracker crumbs
- 1/4 cup sugar
- 1/2 cup melted unsalted butter

for cake:

- 32 oz cream cheese (full fat)
- 1 cup white sugar
- 3 Tbs all purpose flour
- 5 eggs
- 1 tsp vanilla extract
- 1 tsp lemon zest
- 1/3 cup heavy cream

for topping:

- 1 cup sour cream
- 1/2 tsp vanilla extract
- 2 Tbs white sugar

Directions

Mix crumbs, sugar and butter, spread into bottom and up about 1" up the sides of a 10" springform pan (coat pan with cooking spray if it is not nonstick). Press crumb crust in firmly and place in freezer while you make the cream cheese filling. Combine cream cheese with sugar and flour and beat together well, add eggs, one at a time, beating after each addition. Add cream, vanilla extract and stir to combine.

Pour cheesecake mixture into springform pan, place on a large baking pan and put in a preheated 350 oven for 15 mins. Lower oven temp to 250 and continue to bake for 1.5 hours or until cheesecake is almost completely set. Remove from oven and place on a wire rack.

Combine sour cream, sugar and vanilla and spread over the top of the warm cheesecake. Return to oven for 15 mins. Turn oven off, and open oven door, let cheesecake cool slowly in oven for 30 mins. Remove from oven, carefully run a knife around edge to loosen and help prevent cracking and cool completely to room temp. Topping will look prettier after refrigeration. Cover cheesecake with plastic wrap and refrigerate at least 8 hours and up to two days. Cheesecake freezes very well, to freeze wrap well in heavy duty foil or plastic wrap, thaw in refrigerator.

CHERRY COOKIES

Super easy yet beautiful cookie recipe, wonderful to add a touch of color to holiday cookie platters.

Ingredients

- 1 cup softened unsalted butter
- 1/2 cup sugar
- 1/4 cup light corn syrup (can use honey instead)
- 2 egg yolks
- 1/2 tsp vanilla extract
- 2.5 cups all purpose flour
- 10 oz jar Maraschino cherries, halved (or candied cherries)

Directions

Cream together sugar and butter until light and fluffy. Add corn syrup, egg yolks, extract and beat well. Add flour, a little at a time until dough is mixed well. Cover and refrigerate for 1 hour.
Shape dough into 1 inch balls. Roll balls in sugar, use end of a wooden spoon to make an indentation in each cookie. Place 1/2 of a maraschino cherry in each depression. Bake at 325 F on parchment lined baking sheets for 14-16 minutes. Cool on a wire rack.

CHOCOLATE BISCOTTI

Decadent, easy low fat cookies which keep amazingly well.

Ingredients

- 1.5 cups all purpose unbleached flour
- ½ cup unsweetened high quality cocoa powder
- 1 tsp baking powder
- ½ tsp salt
- 1 cup sugar
- 2 eggs
- 1 tsp vanilla extract
- 1 cup dried cranberries (or cherries) chopped coarsely

Directions

Preheat oven to 350 F. Beat eggs, sugar and vanilla with mixer for 3 mins, until pale and thick. Sift together flour, cocoa and salt. Add to egg mixture. Stir to combine and add in cranberries. Line a cookie sheet with aluminum foil. Divide dough in half and with moistened hands shape each half into a 12" log, spacing the logs about 2" apart on cookie sheet (Note: dough will be very sticky, wet hands helps). Bake for 30 mins. Let cool briefly, using a spatula remove logs from sheet and cut crosswise at a slight diagonal into ½" thick slices. Stand these about ½" apart on baking sheet and return to oven for 10 mins for slightly chewy cookies or 15-20 mins for harder biscotti. If cookies

www.youtube.com/ilovetocookalot

will not stand, lay flat on baking sheet and turn over half way through cooking time. Remove to wire rack to cool completely. Can store in an airtight container for up to 2 weeks.

DARK CHOCOLATE BROWNIES

Decadent and rich brownies, made using 99% unsweetened pure dark chocolate - so good.

Ingredients

- 4 oz 99% high quality unsweetened chocolate
- 6 tbs unsalted butter
- 1.5 cups superfine sugar
- 3 eggs
- 1 tsp vanilla extract
- 2/3 cup all purpose unbleached flour

Directions

Preheat oven to 350, grease or spray a 9 in x 9 in glass baking pan and line the bottom with parchment paper. Place a medium stainless steel bowl over, not in, a pot of simmering water (or use a double boiler) add chocolate and butter to bowl and stir until chocolate and butter have melted. Remove from heat. Add the sugar to the chocolate mixture and stir to combine. Add the eggs, one at a time, stirring to incorporate fully each egg. Add the vanilla and flour and mix until thoroughly blended. Pour the batter into the prepared pan and bake until a silver knife (or toothpick) inserted in the center pulls out clean, about 25-35 mins. Set on wire rack to cool.

CHOCOLATE CRINKLE COOKIES

Incredible easy and really quick to make, kids can have fun shaping these into balls and rolling in sugar. The dough is a little sticky, but hands are easy to clean!

Ingredients

- 1 2/3 cup unbleached flour
- ½ cup unsweetened high quality cocoa powder
- ½ tsp salt
- 8 tbs unsalted butter
- 11/4 cups white sugar
- 2 eggs
- 1 tsp vanilla
- ½ cup confectioners sugar

Directions

Preheat oven to 350. Grease two baking sheets. Cream together butter and sugar, beat in eggs, one at a time. Add vanilla and beat well. Sift in flour, cocoa and salt. Stir to combine. It will be a sticky dough. Scoop scant tablespoons of dough into hands and form into balls. Roll each ball in

www.youtube.com/ilovetocookalot

confectioners sugar and place on baking sheets 2 inches apart. Bake for 10-15 mins, or until tops are cracked and cookies look done. Remove from oven and let cool on pan on rack for 10 mins. Remove cookies to cooling rack and let cool completely.

CHOCOLATE PUDDING

Decadent, easy chocolate old fashioned pudding.

Ingredients

- 0.5 cups dark brown sugar, packed
- 3 Tbs Dutch processed cocoa
- 3 oz dark unsweetened chocolate
- 3.5 oz bittersweet dark chocolate
- 3 Tbs cornstarch
- 4 cups milk - divided
- 1 vanilla bean, split
- 4 eggs beaten

Directions

Combine cocoa, brown sugar and chocolate in a heavy bottom sauce pan. Add 1/4 cup milk to cornstarch and blend, set aside. Add remaining 3.75 cups milk into chocolate mixture with split vanilla bean and heat over low heat until chocolate is melted, stirring occasionally.

Add milk/cornstarch mixture and stir - heat 6-8 mins. until mixture begins to thicken. Add a1 Tbs of hot chocolate mixture to beaten eggs, and stir to warm eggs. Add egg mixture to chocolate mixture and cook over medium heat for 2-4 mins stirring constantly until mixture thickens. Remove from heat and pour into 6-8 ramekins, remove vanilla bean. Place wax or plastic paper directly on surface of puddings to prohibit a film from forming and refrigerate

www.youtube.com/ilovetocookalot

several hours or overnight. Serve with whipped cream and garnish with fresh mint if desired.

DARK CHOCOLATE TRUFFLE

A real easy take on chocolate truffles.

Ingredients

- 1/3 cup heavy whipping cream
- 6 Tbs unsalted butter
- 2 cups dark chocolate chips, or 11 oz high quality dark chocolate (62% cacao semisweet or 70% cacao bittersweet)
- 1.5 tsp vanilla extract

Toppings:

- ground toasted almonds,
- unsweetened coconut flakes
- cocoa powder

Directions

Heat cream in top of a double boiler, over not in, simmering water. Add butter and stir to melt. Add chocolate and stir to melt remove from heat and stir in vanilla let cool to room temp, then cover and refrigerate at least 2 hours. Using a round tablespoon, shape into balls and roll in topping of your choice let soften a bit at room temp and serve.

www.youtube.com/ilovetocookalot

CHURROS

A deep fried Mexican delight great with very strong coffee.

Ingredients

- 1 stick (8 Tbs) unsalted butter
- 1 cup water
- pinch of salt
- 1 Tbs sugar
- 1 cup all purpose flour
- 3 eggs
- 1/2 cup sugar mixed with 1 tsp cinnamon
- oil, canola or corn for frying

Directions

Heat butter, salt water and 1 Tbs sugar until boiling, lower heat to a simmer. Stir in flour all at once and continue to stir until mixture forms a dough remove from heat add eggs, 1 at a time stirring until mixture is smooth and glossy. Heat 2" oil to 350 F, using pastry bag and a large star tip pipe four inch lengths of dough into hot oil, turn when brown. Remove when golden on both sides to paper towel lined plate. Roll in cinnamon sugar serve hot or at least warm.

BAKED EGG CUSTARD

A retro classic, this comforting custard is welcome by children of all ages.

Ingredients

- 2 eggs
- ¼ cup sugar
- 2 cups milk, scalded
- 1 tsp vanilla extract
- freshly grated nutmeg

Directions

Combine eggs and sugar in mixing bowl, beat with electric mixer on low speed until just combined. Add milk, at first just a splash and continue to beat to temper mixture. Add remaining milk, ¼ cup at a time, beating to combine. In a heat proof casserole place 6 raminkins. Pour custard mixture through a fine strainer and divide among ramikins. Pour very hot water into casserole dish to come to about half height of custard. Sprinkle with freshly grated nutmeg and bake for 30-40 mins. Let cool in water bath for 2 hours.

FLAN

Very impressive, elegant and easy make ahead dessert.

Ingredients

For Carmel:

- 1/2 cup superfine sugar (or regular)
- 2 Tbs water

For flan:

- 2 eggs, 1 egg yolk
- 1.25 cups whole milk
- 1/4 cup sugar
- 1 tsp vanilla extract

Directions

For caramel:
Heat to boiling, stirring occasionally, once boiling don't stir

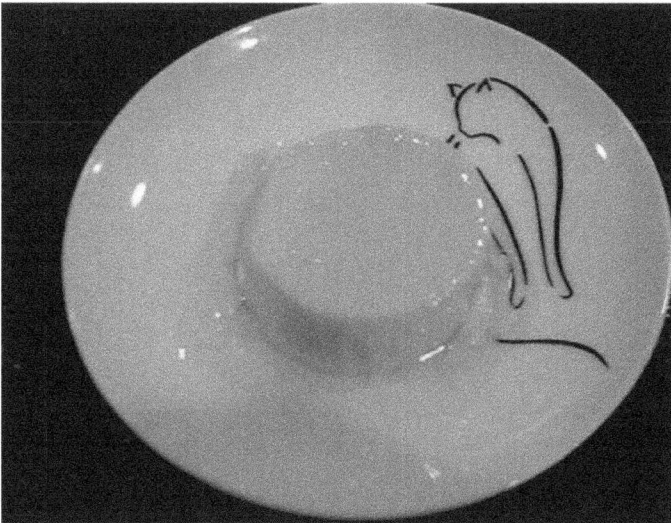

www.youtube.com/ilovetocookalot

watch carefully and remove from heat when sugar turns a golden brown. Pour into three small ramekins, turning to coat

For flan:

Combine 2 eggs, 1 egg yolk beat with mixer, slowly add 1.25 cups scalded milk add 1/4 cup sugar and 1 tsp vanilla extract. Pour into coated ramekins; if you have extra you can make additional custards minus the caramel. Place in a casserole dish and pour boiling water around ramekins, to about the halfway mark. Bake in a 350 F oven for 40 mins or until set. Remove carefully and refrigerate at least 3 hours and up to overnight. Use a knife to loosen flans around edges and invert onto plates. Serve with berries if desired.

FORTUNE COOKIES

Easy to make at home and very popular with children. Make your own good fortune at home.

Ingredients

- 2/3 cup all purpose flour
- 3 egg whites
- 6 Tbs melted unsalted butter
- 1/2 cup sugar
- 1 Tbs cornstarch
- 1 tsp almond extract

Directions

Spray a cookie sheet with cooking spray. Preheat oven to 350 F. Combine all ingredients and whisk together Spread 1-2 Tbs drops of cookies to 3-5 inch rounds, several inches apart on sheet (depending on size of cookie desired) Spread into circle with back of spoon, bake 6-8 mins or until edges are light brown.

www.youtube.com/ilovetocookalot

Working quickly, remove a circle and place fortune (written in food safe ink on a 3"x1/2" strip of clean white paper) in it, fold in half and then fold edges up to form fortune cookie shape. Let cool.

ICE CREAM

A breeze if you have an ice cream maker, and no need to go heavy with the cream. Here are three of my favorite versions. This recipe calls for raw eggs, so make sure to get salmonella free eggs.

Base Ingredients

- 2 large eggs
- ¾ cup superfine white sugar
- 1 cup heavy cream
- 2 cups milk

For chocolate ice cream

- 4 oz unsweetened high quality chocolate

For vanilla ice cream

- 1 vanilla bean, split lengthwise

For peach ice cram

- 2 cups peeled ripe peaches, diced into ¼" chunks
- ¼ cup sugar
- Juice of 1 lemon

Directions

Beat eggs, with wire whisk or electric mixer, until thick and light colored, about 2 mins. Add sugar in small amounts, beating well after each addition. Add vanilla extract. Add milk and cream and stir to combine. For vanilla ice cream, scrape seeds from vanilla bean into ice cream base. Add bean. Refrigerate mixture for several hours and prepare as directed in ice cream maker, removing bean before pouring

www.youtube.com/ilovetocookalot

into machine. For peach ice cream, combine peaches, ¼ cup sugar and lemon juice in small bowl and refrigerate for 1 hour. Stir, drain juice and add to ice cream base. Prepare in ice cream maker as directed adding peaches during last 5 mins of churning. For chocolate ice cream, reserve one cup milk when preparing base. Melt chocolate over a pan of boiling water. Stir in reserved milk and heat gently stirring until smooth. Remove from heat and cool to room temperature. Add to base and prepare as directed in ice cream maker.

JELLY ROLL

Another retro classic, you can mix this up by using your favorite jelly or stabilized whipped cream, or chocolate cream.

Ingredients

- 1/2 cup powdered egg whites
- 1.5 cups warm water
- 3/4 cup white sugar
- 1 cup flour
- 1 tsp vanilla extract
- 2 tsp lemon juice
- pinch of salt
- 1 cup strawberry jelly
- powdered sugar

Directions

Prepare a 10x15 inch jelly roll pan (or baking sheet) by covering with a sheet of parchment paper. Preheat oven to 375 F. Combine egg whites and water and whisk, let sit for a few mins. Beat with a wire whisk attachment for several minutes until stiff peaks form, gradually beat in sugar. Fold in flavorings and flour. Pour out onto baking sheet and spread to an even thickness. Bake about 20 minutes or until golden brown. Carefully peel cake off of parchment

www.youtube.com/ilovetocookalot

paper. Let cool a few minutes. Warm jelly in a small saucepan to thin, spread evenly over cake and roll tightly from long end. Place on a serving tray, seam side down, and sprinkle with powdered sugar. Slice crosswise and serve.

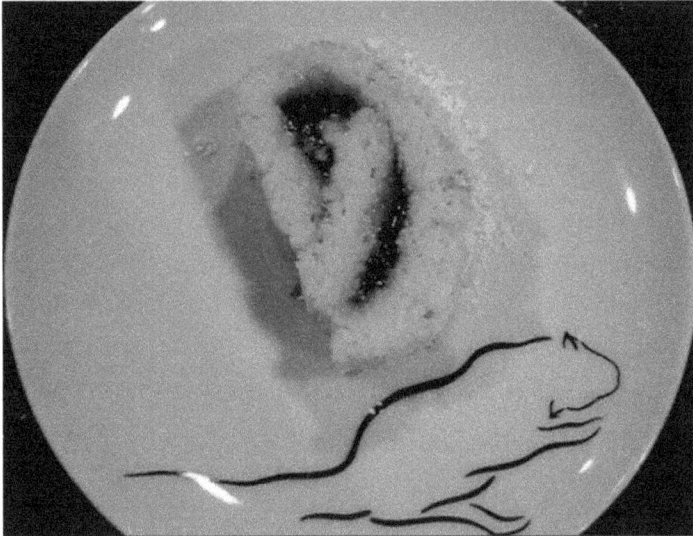

LEMON PIE

Super easy refreshing pie. This is great on a hot summer night.

Ingredients

- 3 egg yolks
- 1 (14 - 15 oz) can condensed milk
- 3/4 cup lemon juice from about 5-6 lemons
- 1 graham cracker crust
- 1 lightly beaten egg white (optional)

Directions

Optionally: brush graham cracker crust with egg white and bake in a 350 F oven for 5 mins. this will make for a crispier crust
Make Filling:
Beat egg yolks and condensed milk together with a hand held mixer for 3 mins until
blended and thick. Slowly add lemon juice beating constantly.
Assemble Pie:
Pour filling into graham cracker crust, and bake at 350 F on a baking sheet, on a center rack oven) for 20-25 mins or

www.youtube.com/ilovetocookalot

until custard is set. Remove from oven and cool on a wire rack for 1 hour.

MADELEINES

A classic French butter cookie. Shaped like a little shell. Refrigerating the batter in the molds helps create the distinctive bump.

Ingredients

- 13 Tbs unsalted butter
- 1 and 2/3 cup confectioners sugar
- 1/2 cup + 1 Tbs all purpose flour
- 1/2 cup finely ground unblanched almonds
- 6 large egg whites
- 1 Tbs honey
- Cooking spray, or flour and melted butter for dusting pan

Directions

Prepare the brown butter: in a medium sauce pan over moderate heat melt butter until it turns brown and gives off a nutty aroma. remove to a bowl to arrest cooking. Let cool. Sift the flour and sugar into a bowl and stir in almonds. In a mixer, beat egg whites until frothy. Add flour/sugar/nut mixture and stir. Add honey and brown butter. Spray pan and using a spoon divide 1/2 of mixture into molds, filling nearly to the top. Refrigerate pan for at least 30 mins and up to one hour. Bake at 375 for 12-15 minutes or until golden and springy to the touch. Immediately remove Madeleines from mold and let cool on a wire rack. Let pan cool and spray again then divide remaining batter in pans, refrigerate then bake as in previous batch.

www.youtube.com/ilovetocookalot

PINEAPPLE UPSIDE DOWN CAKE

The full blown butter laden high calorie take on this classic.

Ingredients

- 1/4 cup unsalted butter
- 3/4 cup packed dark brown sugar
- 20 oz can pineapple rings, packed in juice
- 1/2 cup chopped pecans (optional)
- 1.5 cups all purpose flour
- 6 Tbs cake flour
- 6 Tbs ground roasted unsalted almonds
- 1 tsp baking powder
- 1/2 tsp salt
- 2 sticks (1 cup) unsalted butter at room temp
- 1.5 cups white sugar
- 4 eggs
- 1 tsp vanilla extract
- 3/4 cup sour cream
- 8-10 red cherry halves (optional)

Directions

Heat brown sugar and 1/4 cup butter in a small saucepan until bubbly. Pour into bottom of a nonstick 9 inch cake pan. Place pineapple rings in a single layer snugly in bottom of pan on top of brown sugar mixture. Scatter chopped pecans over, if desired. Combine flours, ground almonds, baking powder and salt. In a bowl of standing mixer combine butter and sugar and cream on low speed using paddle attachment. Add eggs, one at a time, stirring after each addition. Add vanilla. Fold in 1/2 of the dry ingredients and 1/2 of the sour cream. Stir to combine, add remaining dry ingredients and sour cream. Stir to blend. Spoon batter into prepared pan and smooth top. Bake in preheated 325 F oven for 1 hour, check after 45 mins. A toothpick inserted into center of cake should come out clean. Let cool on a wire rack for 10-15 mins. Invert on to a desert platter. Add cherries into holes in pineapple rings, if desired. Serve warm or at room temp.

RAINBOW COOKIES

These colorful cookies look great on a holiday platter. They are easy to make ahead of time and store in the refrigerator, an old fashioned icebox cookie. I sometimes call them spumoni cookies.

Ingredients

- 1 cup softened unsalted butter
- 1/2 cup sugar
- 1 tsp vanilla
- 1 pinch of salt
- 1 egg
- 2 1/4 cups flour
- 1/4 cup chopped nuts (walnuts, pistachio, almonds)
- 2 Tbs chopped candied red cherries
- 1 oz pure chocolate (unsweetened) melted

Directions

Cream together butter, sugar, egg, salt and vanilla. Add flour. Divide dough into 3 parts
into one part add cherries, into another part add chocolate and more flour if needed, into the
last part add nuts and green food coloring if desired. Line a 9x5x3 inch loaf pan with either parchment paper or aluminum foil down the bottom and up the ends of the pan. Layer the dough in evenly, first the cherry dough, then the chocolate and then the nut dough. Fold the parchment or foil over the dough and cover with plastic wrap. Refrigerate

for at least 4 hours, and up to 6 weeks. When ready to make carefully remove the layered dough from the pan, and remove foil or paper. Slice into 1/4 inch thick slices then slice in halves or quarters and bake on an ungreased cookie tray at 350 F for 10 mins or until the bottoms are browned. Cool on a wire rack.

PEARS POACHED IN MARSALA WINE

Gorgeous and a great make ahead dessert for company, try the wine for a deep red version.

Ingredients

- 2-6 firm bosc pears
- 2.5 cups marsala wine (or red wine or hard cider)
- 0.25 cups superfine sugar
- 0.5 vanilla bean
- 1.5 cinnamon sticks
- 1 Tbs cornstarch
- 1 Tbs cold water

Directions

Peel pears, but leave stem intact. Slice a thin slice from bottom so pears can stand upright, do not core. Place pears in a single layer in a casserole dish that has a lid. Preheat oven to slow (250 F). Pour marsala over pears. Sprinkle with sugar and add vanilla bean and cinnamon sticks. Bring to a simmer over a medium flame. Cover dish and place in oven, after 1.5 hours remove and turn pears over. Return to oven for 1.5 hours. Remove from oven, carefully move pears to serving dish. Remove cinnamon sticks from poaching liquid, remove vanilla bean and squeeze seeds into dish. Mix cornstarch with cold water to blend. Add to poaching liquid and bring to a boil over medium high heat, whisking constantly. Boil while stirring for 1 min. Let cool to lukewarm, and then spoon sauce over and around pears.

Chill several hours. Serve as is, or with vanilla ice cream, creme fraiche or vanilla yogurt.

POUND CAKE

The real deal!

Ingredients

- 1.75 cups sifted cake flour
- 1 cup superfine sugar
- 1/2 tsp salt
- 2 tsp baking powder
- 12 tbs melted unsalted butter
- 4 eggs
- 1/2 cup whole milk
- 1 tsp vanilla extract

Directions

Sift together dry ingredients. Cool melted butter and bring eggs to room temperature. Beat eggs, butter, milk and extract together add sifted dry ingredients and whisk to blend. Pour into a greased and floured 8 x 4 inch loaf pan and bake at 350 F for 50 - 60 mins.

RICE PUDDING

A healthy, yet decadent desert.

Ingredients

- 3/4 cup white rice, medium grain
- 1.5 cups water
- pinch of salt
- 2 cups milk, divided
- 1/4 tsp salt
- 2/3 cup superfine sugar
- 2/3 cup golden raisins
- 1 egg. beaten
- 1 tsp vanilla extract
- 1 Tbs unsalted butter

Directions

Bring water to a boil, add rice and pinch of salt. Lower heat, cover and cook for 20 mins. In a medium saucepan combine 1.5 cups milk, sugar, and rice and salt. Heat, stirring often over medium flame for 15-20 mins, or until mixture thickens. Add beaten egg, 1/2 cup milk and raisins and cook 5 mins more. Remove from heat and add vanilla and butter. Stir. Serve warm or at room temp. sprinkled with nutmeg or cinnamon.

www.youtube.com/ilovetocookalot

TARTE TATIN

Wonderful dish, French and delightful - featuring a simple caramel sauce and a delightful puff pastry crust.

Ingredients

- 1 sheet puff pastry (from a 17 oz pkg) thawed
- 5-6 medium apples, such as granny smith, braeburn, Pippens or Macouns
- 1 cup sugar
- 1/4 cup water
- 3 Tbs unsalted butter

Directions

Preheat oven to 375 peel and core apples and slice into 6 - 8 chunks per apple. Roll thawed pastry on a lightly floured board to form an 11 inch square, round edges, prick all over with a fork and refrigerate, covered until ready to use. Combine sugar and water in a 12 inch heavy bottomed skillet and heat, stirring over moderate heat until sugar is dissolved and mixture turns a pale gold color. Continue to heat for a few minutes

more, swirling pan until a deep amber color forms. Remove from heat and stir in butter.

Add apples in concentric circles in a single layer, cut side down. Return to medium heat and cook 12 -20 mins. until apples are tender and caramel is thickened. Remove from heat and place pastry over top, tucking in sides around apples. Bake for 30 - 40 mins.

Remove from oven and let cool for 10 - 15 mins, place a desert plate over pan and using pot holders carefully flip. Replace any apples that stick to pan and pour any remaining caramel over all. Serve warm with ice cream if desired.

STRAWBERRY RHUBARB PIE

Easy classic summer favorite - using tapioca to thicken the filling.

Ingredients

- 2.5 cups cut up ripe fresh strawberries
- 2 cups cut up fresh rhubarb (any tough strings removed - and never use the leaves!)
- 3 Tbs quick cooking tapioca
- 1.25 cups superfine sugar
- 1/8 tsp nutmeg
- 1/4 tsp cinnamon
- 1/4 tsp salt
- rind from an orange, grated
- pie crust (2) for 9" deep dish pie

Directions

Combine berries and rhubarb, sprinkle with tapioca. Stir in sugar and spices and salt. Let sit for 15 mins. Add orange rind. Turn into unbaked pie shell (place on a cookie sheet to help control spillover) .Put top crust on, crimp sides and vent pie but cutting some slits in the top. Bake on a lower rack in a 400 F preheated oven for 30-40 mins. or until fruit bubbles out of vents. Protect crust edges with foil if too much browning occurs.

ITAILIAN CHEESECAKE

Easy – really easy version of this less dense take on cheesecake decadence.

Ingredients

- 2 lbs whole milk ricotta cheese
- 2/3 cup super fine sugar
- 1/3 cup all purpose flour
- 6 eggs
- 2 tsp vanilla
- zest from two lemons
- juice from 1 lemon
- 1 tsp salt

Directions

Butter and flour a 9.5 inch spring form pan. Beat ricotta until smooth, add sugar and flour, vanilla, salt, lemon zest and juice and beat. Add eggs, one at a time and beat until smooth. Pour into prepared pan and bake on middle rack in oven at 300 F for 1.5-1.75

www.youtube.com/ilovetocookalot

hours or until set. Cool on a wire rack. Remove from pan and chill. Dust with confectioners' sugar and serve. (A fresh berry puree is a nice addition to this as a sauce).

TAPIOCA PUDDING

A family favorite.

Ingredients

- 1/2 cup small pearl tapicoa (not instant)
- 2 cups water
- 1/2 cup sugar
- 3 cups milk
- 2 eggs, beaten
- pinch of salt
- 1 tsp vanilla extract

Directions

Soak tapioca in water overnight in refrigerator drain and place in a medium saucepan, add milk, sugar, beaten eggs and salt. Stirring constantly, heat over moderate heat for 15-20 mins until mixture thickens. Remove from heat and add vanilla. Let cool and serve either warm or chilled. Garnish with fresh fruit or whipped cream.

www.youtube.com/ilovetocookalot

OATMEAL LACE COOKIES

Delicate and dainty!

Ingredients

- 1/2 cup butter at room temperature
- 3/4 cup white sugar
- 1 Tbs vanilla extract
- 1/4 tsp salt
- 1/4 cup flour
- 1 and 1/2 cups rolled oats

Directions

Cream butter and sugar with an electric mixer until light and fluffy. Add vanilla, flour and oats. Refrigerate dough for 1 hour. Line a baking sheet with parchment paper and place 1 Tbs size balls of dough 3 inches apart (cookies will spread). Dip a drinking glass in water and then in sugar and use bottom to flatten cookies bake at 350 for 10-12 mins. Watch carefully. Let cookies cool on paper for 1 min. Remove and cool on wire racks.

www.youtube.com/ilovetocookalot

PANNA COTTA

Easy and very elegant dessert similar to a flan with no baking required.
This pairs well with a simple fruit sauce like a berry coulis.

Ingredients

- ¼ cup milk (whole or 2%)
- 1 envelope unflavored gelatin (1/4 oz)
- 2 ¼ cups cream, or half milk and half cream
- ¼ cup confectioners sugar
- 2 tsp vanilla extract

Directions

Soften gelatin in ¼ cup milk by sprinkling over milk in a small bowl. Let sit 10 mins. Heat cream (or cream and milk, I usually use 1 cup heavy cream and 1 ¼ cups milk) and sugar in a small pot over a medium flame. When mixture is very hot add gelatin mixture and whisk constantly until gelatin is completely dissolved, about 5 mins. Add vanilla. Pour into buttered ramekins and refrigerate for at least 4 hours or overnight. Unmold carefully onto pretty plates and spoon sauce over if using.

www.youtube.com/ilovetocookalot

RASBERRY OR BLACKBERRY COULIS

Ingredients

- 2 cups raspberries or blackberries
- ½ cup sugar
- Juice from ½ lemon

Directions

Heat berries with sugar and juice gentle stirring and mashing to release juice. Cool briefly, strain through a fine strainer pressing down on solids to release juice.

FLOATING ISLANDS

Classic and beautiful – a true labor of love made up of three components – caramel, custard and poached meringues. Ile flottante in French, basically islands made of meringues float atop a classic creme anglaise (a vanilla custard like sauce).

Ingredients

For Caramel:

- ½ cup sugar
- ¼ cup water

For crème anglaise

- 5 egg yolks
- ½ cup sugar
- For meringue
- 5 egg whites (NO yolk in whites)
- 2/3 cup sugar
- 2 cups milk
- 1 vanilla bean

Directions

Beat egg whites until stiff, add sugar and continue beating. Heat milk and vanilla bean (split bean and scrape out seeds into milk). Poach large tablespoonful's of meringue in vanilla milk for 2 mins per side, then drain on clean kitchen towel and place in shallow bowl loosely covered in a bowl. Strain milk from poaching and add additional milk to total

2 cups. Return vanilla bean to milk. Heat milk over low hot water over medium heat. Beat egg yolks with sugar, add a small amount of hot milk to egg yolks and stir constantly, then add eggs to hot milk and stir constantly until mixture thickens; never let mixture come to a boil – when mixture reaches 180 F crème is done. To make caramel, combine sugar and water in a heavy bottomed small pot and cook gently until sugar is dissolved, bring to a boil and continue to cook until mixture turns a deep golden color. To serve, place some cream anglaise in each of 6 dessert bowls, float one meringue on top and drizzle with caramel.

STRAWBERRY SORBET

Easy and refreshing healthy dessert.

Ingredients

- 2 lbs strawberries, washed with green stems removed
- 6 Tbs water
- 3/4 cup superfine sugar
- 1/4 tsp salt
- Juice of 1 lemon
- fresh mint, optional

Directions

Make simple syrup:
Combine water, sugar and salt. Heat to dissolve sugar and salt, stirring. Let cool. Puree strawberries in blender, in batches if needed. Add lemon juice to strawberry puree taste strawberry puree and add simple syrup as necessary. Refrigerate puree until cold, at least 4 hours. Follow directions on ice cream maker. Once sorbets is finished, remove from ice cream maker and put in an airtight container in freezer for 2 hours to ripen, served garnished with mint sprigs if desired.

MENU IDEAS FROM THE RECIPES IN THIS BOOK

Starred recipes are not included in this book.

Company Dinner I

- *Cheese Sables, a few cheeses and green grapes*
- *Homemade raviolis*
- *Sausages (hot and sweet Italian, first poached then grilled) **
- *A lovely salad **
- *Homemade garlic bread **
- *New York style cheesecake*
- *Strawberries with sugar and grand marnier **

Company Dinner II

- *A veggie platter with a simple sour cream/cream cheese/herb dip – including pepper rings in many colors (red, green, orange and yellow), carrot sticks, cherry tomatoes, cucumber sticks, broccoli florets and cauliflower florets **
- *Savory palmiers*
- *Tortilla chips and salsa **
- *Arugula bacon cheddar and apple salad*
- *Crispy chicken simply breaded and sautéed in butter **
- *Veal Saltimbocca*
- *Soft Polenta*
- *Parmesan crusted baby zucchini **

www.youtube.com/ilovetocookalot

- *Decadent chocolate brownies*
- *Fresh strawberries macerated in triple sec and confectioners sugar and crème fraiche* *

Backyard get together

- *Chips and salsa* *
- *Chicken and steak fajitas, with guacamole, salsa, sour cream, green onions and cheese* *
- *Savory black beans (canned black beans, with sautéed diced green bell pepper, onion and a little vinegar)*
- *Mexican rice*
- *Red sangria* *
- *Decadent chocolate brownies*

Celebration Dinner I

- *Vadas* *
- *Aloo Goobi*
- *Vegetable Curry*
- *Royal rice*
- *Naan* *
- *Italian cheesecake*

Celebration Dinner II

www.youtube.com/ilovetocookalot

- *Spinach Salad*
- *Veal Canneloni*
- *Apricot Almond Tart*

Large Gathering

- *Veggie platter **
- *Caprese salad*
- *Crispy sausages **
- *Meatballs*
- *Timpano*
- *Lasagnas: spinach, mushroom and meat*
- *Cookie platter*

Snacks with style

- *Mini gourgres*
- *Crostini with assorted toppings like pesto and tapenade*
- *Fresh fruit: green grapes, blueberries, strawberries, thread the fruit on toothpicks **
- *Chocolate chip cookies **
- *Chocolate Biscotti*
- *Almond Biscotti*

Family Dinner I

- *Lasagna al forno*
- *Garden Salad* *
- *Garlic bread* *
- *Three bean salad*
- *Chocolate pudding*

Family Dinner II

- *Fried chicken*
- *Coleslaw*
- *Hush puppies* *
- *Green beans*

Family Dinner III

- *Stuffed grape leaves*
- *Hummus*
- *Pita crisps*
- *Mashed potatoes*
- *Baked acorn squash* *

Easy Weeknight Dinner I

www.youtube.com/ilovetocookalot

- *Wedding Soup*
- *Onion Bread*

Easy Weeknight Dinner II

- *Minestrone*
- *White Bread*

Easy Weeknight Dinner III

- *Beef Broccoli*
- *White Rice ***

Easy Weeknight Dinner IV

- *Chicken Cutlets with Garlic Chard and Spaghetti Squash*

Picnic

- *Tortellini Skewers*
- *Pasta Salad with Tri Colored Roasted Peppers*
- *Onion Sesame Bread*
- *Fried Chicken*

Romantic Dinner

www.youtube.com/ilovetocookalot

- *Veggies (cut up in heart shapes where possible, including red pepper, green pepper, cucumber, carrots, celery) with roasted red pepper dip **
- *Oyster Pan Roast*
- *Grilled Filet Mignon with green peppercorn sauce (perfect steak)*
- *Steamed Asparagus **
- *Heart Shaped mashed potatoes **
- *Red Jello Hearts with whipped cream **

Vegetarian Dinner

- *Eggplant parmesan*
- *Garlic bread **
- *Green Salad **

Thanksgiving

- *Turkey*
- *Spiced cranberry sauce*
- *Chestnut apple stuffing, with or without sausage*
- *Sweet potatoes, candied*
- *Brussels Sprouts*
- *Rolls & gravy **
- *Pumpkin Pie*

Christmas Eve

www.youtube.com/ilovetocookalot

- *Mushroom turnovers*
- *Veggie platter - with cut up red, green bell peppers, cauliflower served with red pepper dip* *
- *Crostini with pesto, garnished with sundered tomato in oil or strips of roasted red pepper*
- *Pirogies*
- *Kilbasa* *
- *Pumpkin Pie*
- *Christmas cookie platter: Rainbow cookies, Chocolate biscotti, Christmas biscotti*

Christmas Breakfast

- *Frittata*
- *Pumpkin Bread*
- *Tropical Fruit Salad with pomegranate seeds*

Christmas dinner

- *Cranberry sauce*
- *Goose fat roasted potatoes* *
- *Roasted Goose* *
- *Green beans with almonds sautéed in butter* *
- *Chestnut stuffing*
- *Bouche de noel* *
- *Biscotti di Regina*

www.youtube.com/ilovetocookalot

New Years Eve appetizer party

- *Cheese Allumettes*
- *Roastedf stuffed mushrooms*
- *Mini Gourges*
- *Roast Beef Spirals*
- *Crostini with Tomato Basil and Garlic topping*
- *Veggie platter of cut up red, green, yellow and orange bell peppers served with dip **
- *Cavier **
- *Floating Islands*

New Year's Eve Formal dinner

- *Parmesan Cheese Straws*
- *Oyster Pan Roast OR asparagus soup*
- *Beef Wellingtons*
- *Roasted Asparagus **
- *Creme Brulee or Pears Poached in Marsala wine*

Dessert party

- *Dark Chocolate Brownies*
- *Madeleines*
- *Cheese Cake, with raspberry coulees*
- *Almond Biscotti*

www.youtube.com/ilovetocookalot

- *Chocolate Biscotti*
- *Apple Crisp with homemade vanilla ice cream*
- *Pineapple Upside down cake*
- *Mini carrot cupcakes*